How to Make & Keep Friends: Helping Your Child Achieve Social Success

How to Make & Keep Friends:
Helping Your Child Achieve Social Success

How to Make & Keep Friends: Helping Your Child Achieve
Social Success

ISBN-10: 1499358806

ISBN-13: 978-1499358803

This book is dedicated to the two best friends and most supportive people in our lives, Jeff Briggs and Michael Quigley.

We are grateful to our editor Rachel Beth Cohen, our illustrator Ryan Flynn, and all of the moms who helped us bring this book to publication.

Contents

Section 2: A Parent's Role as a Social Coach

Section 3: Key Phrases and Coaching Examples

Introduction

Welcome! We are so happy that you found us and this parent companion to the book we wrote for kids, *How to Make & Keep Friends: Tips for Kids to Overcome 50 Common Social Challenges.*

We are social coaches/friendship tutors. In our experience we have found that, while it is important for children to learn manners, social skills go far beyond *please* and *thank you.* In this book we focus on the more difficult skills of initiating, building, and maintaining relationships with peers and friends.

Societal changes have contributed to an increase in the number of kids who struggle with friendships. In the past, kids went outside to play with other neighborhood kids and learned what actions would attract or repel friends there. Kids learned to adapt their behavior to get along in their environment. Over the decades, more households have both parents working, more scheduled lives, and it is no longer as safe in some neighborhoods for kids to play outside and come home when the streetlights come on. Many kids today miss out on the neighborhood experience that supports making and keeping friendships. Fortunately, you have the power to create these experiences for your child, using our coaching tips.

In addition to environmental and schedule changes, technology has also changed the way we interact with one another. Communicating through e-mail, texting, gaming, and social networking has added a layer of complexity to our social structure. As parents, many of us are ill-prepared for the technology that our kids are so skilled at using. It challenges many of us to understand how to guide our kids in this complicated cyber-world. Kids can be vulnerable to negativity in this environment; we need to be able to understand it well enough to teach them *netiquette*, or online manners, in addition to online safety.

These changes, along with an increase in the number of children who are diagnosed with ADHD, social anxiety, and Autism Spectrum Disorders, have broadened and increased the need for social coaching for kids.

As social coaches, we have supported hundreds of children with similar issues. We refer to them as A-Plus kids, or kids who might be described as:

Awesome (plus)
- Anxious
- Autism Spectrum
- ADHD
- Awkward
- Angry

If your child is one of these A-Plus personalities, we can provide tools to assist you in helping him improve his peer interactions. The strategies and tips in this book can also be helpful for kids with mild developmental delay, poor sportsmanship skills, social anxiety, and other social communication challenges.

Our approach is language-based and works very well for kids of all ages with mild to moderate social challenges and strong verbal skills. Children who are non-verbal or who use augmentative and alternative communication (AAC) may also benefit from the strategies in this book. Parents and educators may need to provide education around various types of communication, and any devices should be programmed to include social language. More in-depth information regarding the social use of AAC and other circumstances that may affect the social lives of children (such as a challenging home life, foster care, traumatic brain injury, etc.) may be addressed in a future book but are not addressed in detail in these pages.

Strong social skills are built on a foundation of empathy and respect for others. Our philosophy in teaching social skills to children is to first ensure that they feel they are connected to and a part of the process. Our relationship with each child is critical to social coaching. We want them to understand that we are not going to become angry and punitive when they struggle with friendship skills. We are there to blow the whistle, bring them to the sidelines just as any coach would, give them a, "Hey buddy, let's think about what just happened and see if there's another way to approach this," and then send them back into the game. Our role is to teach them to do better, to help them understand how their actions affect others, and provide simple suggestions to improve and build relationships, all while having a really great time.

You can be that social coach for your own child! While this book is not about the science or research behind why children struggle with social nuances, it does offer concrete strategies and tips that have proven to be successful in our social education programs and have helped many children improve their social skills. Every individual child or situation is different, and not all strategies will work for everyone. We suggest that you try the strategies that you feel comfortable using, and implement the ones that work best for your child.

For ease of reading, we will alternate the masculine and feminine genders when referring to children, as both boys and girls appear in equal number in our social groups. The book is organized into three main sections:

Section 1: Understanding Barriers to Friendships

This section explores the common areas where your child may need social coaching so that he can overcome obstacles to friendship. These challenges include difficulty reading social cues or responding to verbal or non-verbal feedback; the inappropriate or unexpected use of humor or over-silliness; being stuck on a certain topic; lack of flexibility in peer interactions; and more. Because these barriers can lead to friendship difficulties, we offer coaching tips and specific social language suggestions to use to help your child improve his social interactions.

Section 2: A Parent's Role as a Social Coach

In this section we combine concrete suggestions for creating social opportunities for your child with coaching tips and language to prepare for social events. We demonstrate how social coaching can take place simply and naturally in any situation without demeaning or embarrassing your child. We also discuss what to do if your child is resistant to your coaching attempts.

Section 3: Key Phrases and Social Coaching Examples

The last section provides a quick reference guide to our social coaching language and phrases as well as examples of how to use this language when coaching your child.

Many children struggle with social challenges. It is our pleasure to share the many tools that we have in our repertoire that have successfully helped so many kids attain, sustain, and generalize improved social interactions with others into their home, school and community environments. In the book we mention specific applications, visuals, games and other tools that we use for coaching children. These suggestions, lists or free downloads can all be found on our website. All kids are capable of making and keeping friends; for some, it takes a little more specific effort and parental support than others. We hope this book offers you encouragement. Your support can make a tremendous difference for your child.

Donna Shea and Nadine Briggs

Section 1:

Understanding Barriers to Friendships

The lack of acceptance of your child by his peers can break your heart and bring you to tears. If your child is not adept at sports, math, or singing, it is usually not as hurtful because you can simply re-focus on his strengths.

When your child is dismissed as a friend, he is being rejected for who he is as a person, for his personality. It may be more painful for you than it is for your child. This is especially true if your child is not able to read social cues from the children he is trying to have as friends. You might cringe while you watch him continue to try to connect, often making it worse with each attempt.

As parents of children who have struggled socially, we have also personally experienced that pain, and we fully understand this type of parental angst. It is important to understand that you are not alone.

Many kids have difficulty with friendships. These difficulties are driven by common barriers that we see in our work with kids and address in this section. We also offer specific language suggestions at the end of each section to assist you in helping your child overcome these barriers to friendship.

1

Overly Silly Behavior

Barrier: In order to be noticed by his peers, and to satisfy his need for positive feedback from potential friends, a child who experiences social difficulties may engage in frequent attention-seeking, overly silly, behavior. When he gets a laugh in response he will try to get it again, and then again. Each attempt increases both his own level of silliness as well as the chance that other kids will start laughing *at* him. Unfortunately, some kids and many adults will respond with a fake laugh or some other encouragement to spare your child's feelings.

Coaching Suggestion: The fake laugh approach will only encourage your child to continue the behavior and, although considered polite in many circumstances, it is not in the best interest of your child. It is more helpful to say, "I'm confused" or "I really didn't get why that's funny." Ask your child if he can figure out if he is being too silly or just the right amount of silly for the situation. Your child may be overly silly simply because he doesn't know how to:

- Invite someone to play;
- Choose a topic to start a conversation; or
- Join a group or activity.

If the overly silly behavior is persistent, we provide additional tips on how to interact with others in following sections.

Suggested Social Language:

"I guess we enjoy different types of humor."

"I'd like to play with you, but the sillies are making it hard."

"Do you think that there is too much, too little, or just enough silliness going on right now?"

"I don't really understand that joke."

"I'm confused about what is supposed to be funny."

"Can you tell if the other kids are laughing with you or at you when you do that?"

"That was really funny one time, let's move on please."

2

A Harsh Tone of Voice

Barrier: Your child may have trouble hearing her own tone of voice or truly not have any idea that she sounds harsh or irritated. Or she may be aware that her tone is harsh but might not understand the impact that it has on others and on her relationships with them.

Coaching Suggestion: Use the word *that* instead of *you* when describing an unfriendly tone of voice. Examples are:

Do: "*That* sounds angry. What's up?"
Do Not: "*You* are being rude."

Do: "*That* sounds disrespectful. I don't think you meant it to be. How could you say it differently?"
Do Not: "*You* are being disrespectful."

Do: "*That* came across as a little condescending, even though I think you were trying to be helpful."
Do Not: "*You* think you know more than everyone else."

Using the word *you* can create defensive feelings and even begin an argument. When your child is angry or annoyed, allowing her to acknowledge her feelings is a key part of learning empathy. She also needs to learn how to manage those feelings in a social situation. Coaching might sound like this:

"It's okay to feel angry and annoyed. Instead of sharing that feeling with your friends, let's talk about what you can do when you feel this way. How about taking a 3 + 10 break, which is three deep belly breaths followed by counting to 10, or come get me to help if you are not sure how to handle the situation."

16

Suggested Social Language:

"That sounds angry. What's up?"

"That sounded disrespectful, but I don't think you meant it to be. Please try saying it again."

"I understand that you are trying to be helpful, but the tone of voice being used sounds a little condescending."

"That's a pretty frustrated tone of voice. Let's figure out what is frustrating you and see what we can do to fix it."

3

A Preference for Adult Companions

Barrier: It is not typical for kids to prefer to spend time with adults. This preference is likely driven by anxiety about being around other children or general difficulties with peer interactions. You can help this insecurity if you consider why your child may be anxious. Common underlying reasons for social anxiety in your child may be:

- He does not understand the rules of a game.
- He has poor communication skills.
- He does not feel welcome in the group.
- He does not know how to join the group.
- He is worried that he will be rejected.
- He is concerned that he might get bumped too hard by another child during play.
- He is feeling overwhelmed by too many kids.
- He had a bad experience and is holding on to that memory.
- He has difficulty losing.
- He feels more comfortable being with adults.

Coaching Suggestion: Your child cannot, or will not, always express why he is reluctant to join a group of other children. Because of this, it helps to have the reasons listed above in mind when trying to assess *why* your child is reluctant. Offer to review the rules of the game that the other kids are playing, give him the language to join in, and generally support him in his efforts.

This is also an opportunity to teach empathy to the rest of the group. It is always best to ask the other kids to invite your child to join them. The other kids can explain the rules or support the needs of the reluctant child. It is helpful to choose one kid from the group to be the leader in inviting your child to join in and then coach that peer on how to raise your child's comfort level. For example, the peer could ask your child to join his or her team. Chances are the child you assign to this task will think of creative ways to integrate your child into the group. Your child will be more likely to respond positively if the invitation comes from his peers.

Suggested Social Language:

From parent to child:

"Are you worried about something? Let's figure out what it is and come up with some ideas to help."

"Would you like me to explain the rules of the game to you or practice with you first?"

"How about you try one new thing one time for one minute?"

From child to peers: *"I'd like to play with you. What are you doing? instead of Can I play with you?"*

From peers to child:

"We want you to play with us."

"You can be on my team."

4

Not Wanting Friends

Barrier: Your child may seem like she does not want friends. She might even tell you that she does not want friends. This can be especially true of children on the Autism Spectrum or those who are very socially anxious. There are children who are truly happy playing alone. Social coaching is still vital for your child even if friendship is not the initial focus. The ability to get along well with others is an important skill for your child to learn because interactions with other people are unavoidable. Eventually, your child will be required to work in small groups and will have a job where she will participate in meetings and projects. Social skills are a necessary part of life.

Coaching Suggestion: Working to uncover why your child does not want friends is another way to help her to access friendships. It may be due to anxiety or fear of being rejected, or she may have some requirements for friends that she cannot find on his own, but which you could help her find. Peers who do not share the same intellectual or creative interests can become easily bored or annoyed with each other and seek more solitary activities.

Pairing kids with like-minded peers is certainly a great step but not always feasible. Teaching tolerance and patience is also important when dealing with others. To help your child learn tolerance:

- Acknowledge that she may be an expert on a particular topic and encourage her to share a limited amount of her knowledge. This may be enough of a self-esteem boost to keep her aggravation in check;

- Encourage her to understand that everyone has different interests and that others may not share her particular passion;

- Remind her that while she may be very bright in certain subjects, everyone has different forms of intelligence;

- Reinforce that learning to get along and work with other people is an important and unavoidable life skill; and,

- Explain what it means to be a good friend. Refer to the Real Friends Checklist in Section 2.

Suggested Social Language:

"It might help you with other kids to try being more of a generalist than a specialist. How about learning a little bit about popular music, how the local sports teams are doing, or seeing a movie that's out now?"

"I know you don't want to play Sally's game, but it is important to try it for the sake of friendship."

"If there are too many kids, try to play with just one."

"Let's try one new thing today for only a few minutes."

5

Perseverating
(Getting Stuck on a Topic)

Barrier: Perseverating is when your child gets stuck on a particular topic or asks the same type of question repeatedly. Perseverating can be extremely annoying and peers will avoid your perseverating child to remove themselves from the constant questioning. Parents can become impatient with perseverating as well. A perseverative conversation might sound something like this:

Child: "I have a birthday party today."
Parent: "Yes, it's at 1:00."
Child: "I'm so excited!"
Parent: "I know. Birthday parties are exciting."
Child: "What time is it now?"
Parent: "9:00"
Child: "I have a party today. I'm excited about my party. I'm going to a birthday party. I don't want to miss it. What time is it now?"
Parent: "9:05"
Child: "I'm going to have cake and there will be presents! What time is it?"
Parent: "9:07"
Child: "We'll play games and have fun."
Parent: "Yes, parties are such fun."
Child: "Who is going to bring me? Can we go the party now?"
Parent: "Not until 1:00."
Child: "But I have a party."
Parent: "Yes, we'll take you when it's time to go."
Child: "But I want to go now. Why can't I go now?"
Parent: "They aren't ready for you to come this early."
Child: "When is it 1:00?"

Parent: "We'll go right after lunch."
Child: "Can I have lunch now?"

Coaching Suggestion: Tell your child that his question was already answered and then ask him to repeat the answer that was already given. If you feed the need by answering the questions repeatedly, it may encourage the perseverating to continue. Instead, try responding with, "We just covered that. Why don't you tell me what comes next?"

Acknowledge that he is stuck by saying, "It sounds like your brain is stuck on that topic. Let's move on to something else." Attempt to stop the perseverating by simply and gently saying, "We're all done discussing that now." The thought process of perseverating is similar to obsessive compulsive disorder (OCD). The more a compulsion is fed, the more strength it gets. You have the ability to cut off the food source, so to speak. As with many of the topics in this book, we have personally dealt with this issue as parents. Our advice, while perhaps more parental than clinical, has been effective nonetheless.

Suggested Social Language:

"I think you might be worried about something."

"Let me write this down for you."

"It sounds like your brain is stuck on that topic. I want to move on to something else."

"We are done discussing that for now."

"How about you tell me the answer?"

"Asked and answered."

6

Self-Talk

Barrier: Your child may use self-talk as a way to process information. It is a great processing tool, when appropriate and needed, but she should be taught boundaries about when and where it is okay.

Coaching Suggestion: Try to be very gentle in your coaching on this issue because the reason for self-talk is to process life's input. Point out, "It confuses those around you if they do not know who you are talking to." It helps to put the confusion on everyone else rather than making your child feel that she is doing something wrong. It helps to say, "There is nothing wrong with talking to yourself as long as it is done in private." Because this can be interpreted in different ways, follow up with a clarification of what you mean by private. For example, the stall in a public bathroom is only semi-private and the thoughts expressed during that activity should not be shared publicly.

Suggested Social Language:

"I hear your private thoughts leaking."

"It confuses people around you if they do not know who you are talking to."

"There is nothing wrong with talking to yourself as long as it is done in private."

"We need to work at keeping some of those thoughts inside your head."

7

Shyness or Anxiety

Barrier: Your child may experience shyness of varying degrees. He may just be uncertain of how to join a group or he could experience social anxiety at a level that makes even simply speaking in public a challenge.

Coaching Suggestion: Encouraging small moments of bravery is a great strategy for helping your child overcome shyness. Expecting large gains may be too intimidating for kids who are shy and might result in a setback. Even though parents have the best of intentions, forcing your shy child to interact is one of the least effective means of engaging him. It shines a social spotlight on your child and typically causes more withdrawal. We suggest you refrain from demanding your child say hello, forcing him to join a group, or insisting that he converse with people who are not well known to him. Give your child permission to feel shy in different settings, and assure him that he is going to have a safe and fun time. Try observing activities with your child, from a distance, until your child feels comfortable enough to join the group. Engaging another child to come over to invite your child to play can also be effective.

Most children who are shy are usually just slow to warm up and will gradually join in. Go slowly with your child so he does not feel pushed. Encourage manners, and explain what the expectations are in different settings, but if your child is not responding, or begins to shrink further into himself (or behind your leg), drop it and move on to something else.

With very shy children, or those with a diagnosis of selective mutism, it is important to consider that your child may have an underlying anxiety issue. We highly recommend the book *Growing Up Brave* by Dr. Donna

Pincus. It offers excellent suggestions on how you can help children address and master anxiety.

Children who are anxious benefit from understanding what anxiety feels like. Here are some physical descriptors of anxiety that can be helpful to share with your child:

Blushing
Lump in throat
Butterflies
Pain in the chest
Shortness of breath
Irritability
Sweaty palms
Stomachache
Heart beats fast
Tingly feelings
Weakness
Feeling like vomiting

Blurry vision
Feeling smothered
Ringing in the ears
Diarrhea
Tightness in chest
Being mean
Headache
Feeling dizzy
Being tearful
Feeling cold
Nausea
Shakiness

Suggested strategies to cope include:

- Teaching your child that anxiety is generally based on *what if* thinking and not on facts;
- Focusing on his strengths and reminding him that those are more powerful than his worries;
- Encouraging him to focus on what he can do and then highlighting his accomplishments;
- Demonstrating how to confront and cope with worries by analyzing whether the concern is probable or just possible; and,
- Teaching him to power through events that he finds stressful and to resist the urge to back away from his fears.
- Identifying someone your child respects and suggesting that he manage his worry the way that person would.

- Creating encouragement cards with reaffirming statements that may be reviewed during stressful times.
- Suggesting that he try taking three deep belly breaths.
- Encouraging him to change the channel in his mind and imagine good things instead.
- Creating a worry box and telling him to put his worries in the box to discuss with you or another trusted adult when he has the opportunity.
- Praising gently when your child overcomes his fears (but be sure not to overly praise since this could cause further anxiety).

Teach your child that his choices make him powerful, and that he has control over his thoughts. We like to tell children that they have the courage of a lion inside even though they may feel like a kitten. This provides a nice visual image for them to help find courage within themselves.

In coaching your shy child, you should also take note of your own anxiety and not feed into your child's anxiety. If you are a protective helicopter parent when your child is acting particularly shy (answering questions for him, lingering when it is time to separate, etc.) you are not giving your child the opportunity he needs to overcome his shyness.

Suggested Social Language:

"It's okay to feel shy."

"Are you worried about something?"
"Are you wondering what to expect?"

"Is your worry the right amount for the situation?"

"It's okay to watch the other kids for a few minutes before you try it."

"What's the worst that can happen?"

"Did anything bad happen the last time?"

"Let's try one new thing, one time, for one minute."

"How about focusing on just one person in the group rather than everyone at once?"

8

Bossy and Demanding Behavior

Barrier: If we are being honest, we would acknowledge that we ALL would like to have our own way ALL of the time, but that is just not the reality of living, playing, and working with other people. If your child is adamant about controlling play with her peers, or demanding things be done a certain way, she will quickly find herself involved in conflicts, or even with no one to play with at all.

Coaching Suggestion: When you hear a bossy-sounding statement coming from your child, there is a simple intervention that usually works like magic (and we tell kids that these are the magic words of friendship). Coach your child to exchange the words, "You have to" for "How about we?" Explain that these words give each person the chance to share their ideas and it starts the process of problem-solving toward a mutual solution.

If you find your child continues to be rigid in her thinking and still wants to control the play, then take it a step further and explain to her the probable consequences of this barrier. It can be very powerful asking your child, "Do you want to have friends?" (Most kids will say, "Yes.") Then say, "Let's think about what's not working and see what you might be able to do instead." At this point, your child will likely allow you to partner with her and to teach her the friendship skills she needs.

Suggested Social Language:

"That sounded a little bossy. Let's try the magic words and say, 'How about we (fill in the blank)?' instead."

"How about we consider your friend's idea, too?"

"Let's let her ideas play, too."

"Nice gets nice or treat others the way you want to be treated."

"Let's do it your way first, and my way next."

"I don't think that your friend's ideas are being heard."

"Let's catch this small problem and solve it before it turns into a big one."

9

Aggressive Behavior

Barrier: If your child struggles with aggressive behaviors, it presents a unique challenge in building friendship skills. Aggression, and the need to keep your child and those around him safe, are issues that need to be addressed before interactive social coaching with peers can be successfully undertaken.

In defining aggression, we differentiate between a child who might push someone on the playground out of frustration in an isolated incident and a child whose anger and aggression are so severe that they cause fear in those around him. If your child exhibits consistent and frequent aggressive tendencies, it is important to discuss this with your pediatrician or to engage the help of a mental health provider. However, isolated incidents of minor aggression can usually be addressed by teaching your child the skills and strategies he needs to manage his frustration and anger.

Coaching Suggestion: Explain to your child that it is perfectly normal for him to feel angry at times but that it is not okay to hurt others, himself, or property. Kids exhibiting minor aggression (for example, pushing or pinching) need to be taught more effective responses to situations that frustrate them. If your child uses minor aggression as a form of problem solving, teach him how to resolve conflict during a time when he is calm. Teach him how to compromise, suggest that he rate the importance of the problem he is facing, recommend that he take a break when needed, and help him to practice self-soothing techniques such as three deep belly breaths or counting to ten. The key is for him to be able to use these strategies to help manage his feelings before they get too intense to control.

Here is an example of how to handle minor aggressive behavior. If two children are arguing over a toy, resulting in one of the children getting hit or pushed, social coaching the altercation might go like this:

Parent: "Hey, whoa there! I can see two very frustrated people having an argument over this truck. Let me hold it for a minute (taking the truck). What's going on?" (Avoid mentioning the hitting.)

Nick: "I had that truck first!"

Matthew: "No you didn't. I had it first!"

Nick: "Did not!"

Matthew: "Did too!"

Parent: "Okay guys. I can see that two people want the same toy, and there is only one. That's a bummer. I'm wondering if we can figure out what to do about this."

Nick: "We could share it."

Matthew: "But I had it first!"

Parent: "I didn't see who had it first, so I'm sorry about that. We still only have the one truck and two people who want to use it. Is there a way we could figure out how to take turns with it? I really don't want to have to put it away but might have to if it's causing too much trouble today."

Matthew: "Oh, alright. We can take turns. But I want to go first!"

Parent: "I'm sure you do Matt, but I'm sure that Nick wants it first, too. Let's first figure out how long a turn should be. What do you guys think?"

Nick: "Three minutes!"

Parent: "Matthew, is three minutes okay for you? I have my timer here so we can keep track."

Matthew: "Three minutes is okay. But I want to go first!"

Parent: "Looks like we need to solve tha, too. How can we decide who goes first?"

Matthew: "Rock, paper, scissors?"

Parent: "Great idea Matthew! Now what are you guys going to do if the other guy gets to go first instead of you?"

Nick: "Wait for the three minutes?"

Parent: "Sounds good to me. Looks like Nick won and is having the first turn. I'm setting the timer for Matthew's turn, and we can keep switching for as long as you both want turns. Now, before I give the truck to Nick, do you see how this was a much better way to work out a problem with a friend rather than hitting him? Great. Now go have some fun together."

When your child becomes aggressive, the first reaction is often to punish or, in this example, to make him give the toy back, or any other number of solutions that do not work. Why do they not work? Because your child's brain is stuck on the problem at hand and is not available for you to teach him a different way of going about getting what he needs or wants. Teaching is the true definition of discipline. If you stop to take the time to teach you are instilling in him skills that he can use, rather than continually disciplining the same behaviors over and over again.

Suggested Social Language:

"Is this a big deal or a little deal?"

"I'm here to help you handle this."

"Let's catch your anger before it gets you in trouble."

"Your brain is starting to feel angry. Give it three deep breaths."

"Let's solve the problem before it gets too big."

10

Impulsive Behavior

Barrier: You may have a child who is impulsive, or the "ready, fire, and *then* aim" type, who frequently finds herself dealing with angry peers. A secondary challenge that your child might have is that she is not reading social feedback or understanding the consequences of her impulsive action. Typical examples of impulsive behaviors that your child might exhibit are:

- Grabbing something out of someone else's hands;

- Asking if she can have something while she is already taking it;

- Jumping into the middle of a game in a "bull in a china shop" fashion;

- Continuously moving someone else's game piece despite being repeatedly asked not to do so;

- Blurting out or interrupting others; and,

- Being physically aggressive.

Coaching Suggestion: The key to helping your impulsive child is letting her know that you understand that she does not *mean* to do these things; she just has a brain that has a hard time slowing down to stop and think first.

Instead of meeting your impulsive child's actions with anger, simply say, "Was that one of those things that happened before your brain had a chance to stop and think?" There will likely be a look of visible relief on her face. From there, have a discussion about impulsiveness and the strategy of trying to visualize a stop sign in her brain to help her stop and think. Another strategy to use is to talk to her about "freezing" her brain and body. Play freeze tag to practice this strategy outside of challenging situations.

Your child who is impulsive lives in the moment of action and doesn't stop to consider the consequences of her actions. She may even be surprised that a consequence happens. Work with your child about the need to pre-think an action, just for a split second, before she executes his idea. Remind her that it will save her having to re-think a mistake after it happens.

It may be helpful to understand that children who struggle with impulsivity could have a social maturity level that may be up to one third less than their chronological age. We recommend basing expectations on functional age versus chronological age.

Impulsiveness is often an indicator of ADHD in children. If your child does or may possibly have ADHD, you, her teachers, and anyone else who is interacting with her should view impulsiveness from the lens of a *symptom* and not a *behavior*. No amount of discipline, behavior plans, reward systems, or social coaching can physically change your child's neurology. It is no easier for your child with ADHD to control her symptoms than it is for a child who has asthma. Your child with ADHD needs understanding (and sometimes medical intervention) along with strategies and support, not punishment for the symptoms of her diagnosis.

Suggested Social Language:

"Was that one of those things that happens before your brain has a chance to stop and think?"

"Freeze your brain."

"Freeze your body."

"If you pre-think what might happen next, what will that help you decide to do instead?"

"I know you didn't mean that. Let's do a do-over."

11

Rigid Thinking

Barrier: If your child struggles with being flexible, he may be tagged as a poor sport or no fun to play with by other kids. Peers will quickly abandon playing with a child who only wants things his own way. He may often exclaim "You're cheating!" or "That's not fair!" Perhaps he cannot see another person's perspective, opinion, or point of view.

Coaching Suggestion: Try this exercise if your child has difficulty being flexible. Give your child several pipe cleaners. Ask him if it is more fun to play with them when they are rigid and straight, or if they can be bent and molded. In the same way, he would be more fun to play with when he chooses to *bend his brain,* rather than being rigid and uncompromising. You may also use the same coaching technique we recommend for bossy-sounding kids, replacing the words "You have to" with "How about we?" to teach the art of compromise.

Acknowledging when your child is using flexible thinking skills is important. Letting him know that you can see him trying, or that he is doing well, reinforces the change in your child's interactions. "I just noticed that you agreed to try something Billy's way. That's terrific!" or, "I heard you say 'how about we?' Great job!" Point out to your child how things work much better for him when he plays interactively instead of rigidly.

Suggested Social Language:

"How about we…?" or *"In my opinion…"* or *"I think…"*

"Is it a big deal or little deal?"

"Let's think about what your friend wants, too."

12

Unique Interests

Barrier: Your child may be one of those children who has a very unique interest in or intense passion for a particular item or topic. The topic can run the gamut from sprinkler systems to vacuum cleaners to the more mainstream interests such as Pokémon™ or Minecraft™. Your child may have vast knowledge about a certain subject such as history, astronomy, reptiles, or video games. Problems start when your child has difficulty talking about anything but her own fascination, and cannot gauge another's attentiveness or adjust to the fact that other people might not be as absorbed as she is. This can cause her peers to become quickly bored and to look for a different playmate.

Coaching Suggestion: Encourage your child to assess the interest level of the person with whom she is conversing to determine how interested the other person will be in the conversation. For example, she could say "Do you like dinosaurs a little or a lot?" She can then adapt how much she discusses dinosaurs based on the answer.

It is not the goal in coaching your child to change her personality or dismiss her uniqueness. However, whether we agree with it or not, society does have certain expectations of its members. In socially supporting your child, it is your job to do several things to address those expectations. One is to find a safe space for her to go and play, be herself, and comfortably interact with like-minded peers and friends. You can search for activities in your own community that fit with your child's interests so that she can meet potential friends that way. If none of these activities exist, create your own! We share our ideas about how to do this in Section 2.

She will also need to be taught that, in certain venues or social scenarios, she will benefit from blending in rather than sticking out. Let her know that even you have to blend in at certain times, including at work and social events. For example, you would not wear an evening gown or a tuxedo to a casual barbecue, or a bright red dress or shirt to a funeral.

If your child does want to let her uniqueness shine, she should be coached on how to do that with her eyes wide open. As an example, your 5th grade daughter who loves super heroes may want to wear her superhero cape to school every day. If she wants to do that, she should be coached on making that choice. Coach her to let her know that, if she does decide to wear it every day, she will be sticking out and will undoubtedly receive some negative social feedback from the kids at school. She may even put herself in a position to be bullied or ostracized.

Your child may demonstrate strong self-esteem and be comfortable enough with her uniqueness to weather a storm of negative feedback and wear the cape. Or she may decide that she is not prepared for that criticism, and may opt to blend in and save the superhero cape for the safety of home.

Explain that, as awesome as it is for your child to be a specialist in one area, many times it is important to be more of a generalist in order to converse with a variety of people. Encourage your child to know a little bit about current movies, current music, popular video games, sports teams, TV shows, and the like, so that she is not lost when other kids are discussing those topics.

Suggested Social Language:

"Are you sticking out or blending in?"

"Are you saying that because <u>you</u> want to say it or because you think others are interested in hearing it?"

"We're wearing out this topic."

"Let's talk about something else now."

"It's time to use a topic-switching statement now." (Provide examples, including: "and on another topic", "to change the subject", "before I forget", "that made me think of", or "I know I'm changing the subject but…")

"Now might be a good time to be more of a generalist than a specialist."

13

Misunderstanding Personal Space

Barrier: Lack of awareness of personal space and boundaries is very common in socially struggling children. He may not mind when someone is close to him, and consequently does not realize when he is intruding on someone else. He may stand or sit too close to others, look over someone's shoulder, reach and grab into someone else's personal area, or walk right through a game or activity. On the flip side, he may need a lot of personal space and does not know how to react when someone else is being invasive.

Coaching Suggestion: In coaching your child about personal space, say something simple, such as, "I think Jimmy is trying to tell you something with his body by leaning away. What do you think that might be?" Explain to your child that everyone has an invisible fence surrounding them or an invisible square in front of them when working at a table or desk. He can figure out when he has crossed that boundary by watching to see if the other person leans away or steps away. A good frame of reference is to stay an arm's length away while standing and a forearm's distance apart when sitting.

For your child who needs personal space you can suggest that instead of getting upset with someone, he can say something like, "I need a little more space, please."

Suggested Social Language:

"I need a little more space, please."

"Notice where your body is and where your feet are stepping."

"I'm not seeing any daylight between the two of you."

"Can you see what your friend's body is saying to you?"

"I think that you might have reached into your friend's invisible square without asking permission first."

14

Holding Grudges

Barrier: Your child may have a very strong sense of justice or rigid thinking. She might hold on to grudges or seek revenge beyond what other children may find acceptable. She may also seek to make things *even*. Not being able to let go of slights could lead to friendship issues and should be addressed.

Coaching Suggestion: Coaching an issue such as this will take perseverance and gentle consistency. It is important to help your child understand the social price she is paying for holding on to a grudge. Helpful coaching approaches include:

- Suggest that she remember that nobody is perfect;

- Explain why she can forgive others even if something was done on purpose;

- Remind her that *she* has needed forgiveness from others in the past, and to consider how she would have felt if forgiveness had not been granted;

- Encourage her that it is time to let go; and,

- Show her how to write down grudges on an index card, rip them up, and throw them out or write and rip up a "no-send" letter.

Suggested Social Language:

"Is it more important to be right or to be happy?"

"Can you tell me how that solves the problem?"

"What would you think if Brianna told you that she didn't want to be your friend anymore?"

15

Disrespect for Others

Barrier (also see: Harsh Tone of Voice): Rudeness and disrespect will certainly have a negative impact on your child's relationships. He may not be aware that he sounds abrasive or that he is not considering the views of others. Assume that your child does not know that he is being rude and bring it to his attention.

Coaching Suggestion: Teaching your child to understand someone else's perspective will also take time and patience but, with persistence, your child can learn this skill. He needs to understand that he will get from his peers what he gives to them. To extinguish purposeful disrespectful behavior, simply ignoring it can sometimes be an effective strategy. You might also point out, "That sounded disrespectful and I'm sure you didn't mean it to be. Try saying it again."

Your child may have a hard time with the language of feelings, and understanding what he does or says causes others to feel. We find it more helpful to ask a child what the other person might be *thinking* instead.

Suggested Social Language:

"What do you think Joey is thinking when you talk to him like that?"

"I see an annoyed look on Karen's face. Can you guess what she might be thinking?"

If a child is being purposefully disrespectful, try:

"When I am being treated nicely, then I will play with you."

"Nice gets nice (and mean gets mean)."

"That sounded a little rude. Would you like to say it again?"

"I don't like it when ____."

16

Lack of Empathy

Barrier: Your child may have a difficult time noticing if someone is sad or upset and then taking appropriate action. Caring for others or expressing that she cares may not come naturally to her. This social skill can be taught by focusing on:

- Asking about and responding to other people's feelings;

- Reading facial expressions and body language;

- Understanding or attending to tone of voice;

- Offering assistance; and

- Complimenting others.

Coaching Suggestion: Empathy can be taught to your child using in-the-moment social coaching. You can help your child learn to identify body language and facial expressions. Questions such as, "Maggie's face looks sad. What should you do?" or "Can you guess what Maggie is thinking right now? How can you help?" The child who struggles with empathy may not want to stop what she is doing to check in on someone in distress. Gentle reminders such as, "It is important to be a good friend and see if you can help," may prompt a child into action. When your child does, in fact, check in on someone or show empathy when prompted, always follow up with praise for her caring and being a great friend.

Playing emotions charades or making an emotions collage are useful ways to help your child understand the emotion behind facial expressions. Eventually, this helps your child understand the effect one's own facial expressions can have on someone else's feelings. Movies and TV shows may also be paused to allow discussion about how to interpret facial expression, tone-of-voice, and body language.

Suggested Social Language:

"Maggie's face looks sad. It's important to ask, 'are you okay?'"

"I don't think you noticed that your friend's face looks upset. You should check in and see if there is anything you can do to help."

"When Mary asks you if you like her picture, she is expecting you to give her a compliment, even if you really don't like the picture."

17

Poor Sportsmanship

Barrier: Losing at games or sports can be supremely challenging for your child. His driving need to go first and/or win can turn an otherwise fun activity into a battleground. As soon as a game starts, the tension may start to rise and the fun begin to fade when your child becomes overly competitive. He may choose not to play games at all because he is not able to handle losing. Games are meant to be a fun part of growing up. Learning good sportsmanship can bring back the fun.

Coaching Suggestion: Reminding your child that games and sports are meant to be fun and that sometimes he will win and sometimes other kids will win, can help set the stage for success. He might equate winning and having fun as the same thing so he may need support to help shift his thinking.

Putting some perspective around losing at a game is an effective way to help your child understand that he may be giving winning too much weight. Talk about various significant topics (for example, a pet is quite ill and has to see a vet) and ask if winning at a game is more or less important.

Previewing the rules to make sure he understands them can avoid conflict later around issues of how the game should be played. Watch for your child trying to change or complicate the game, or attempting to create his own new rules in the middle of the game. Remind him that new rules are fine as long as everyone agrees. Make sure the new rules are not only for his advantage. If new rules are not agreed upon by a consensus, then the rules on the box or the official rules on the Internet are the ones to follow. Try saying, "I understand that everyone likes to win. I like to win, too! The problem is, not everyone can win every time so it is important to let others have a chance."

It is important to help your child understand the difference between games of skill and games of luck. Try to make it fun to lose in a game of luck – cheer on a perfect losing streak. Talk to your child about learning to *fail with flair* or *get "out" with grace.*

You can also help your child learn to play games *strategically* instead of *revengefully.* When every move in a game is strategic, it is much easier to play fair, manage frustration, and avoid arguments.

If cheating occurs, remind your child that being trustworthy is extremely important in friendships. Ask him what he would think if his friends cheated. Remind him that cheating is dishonest and that winning should not be more important than his friendships. Otherwise, it will be hard to keep friends.

Suggested Social Language:

"What would be the strategic move to make?"

"Is winning more important than friendship?"

"If you are going to fail, you might as well fail with flair!"

"Let's practice getting out with grace.

"Let's do a do-over."

"Let's go over the rules."

"Are you going to be okay if I win? How are you going to handle it if you lose?"

"Let's try to keep this fun and not take it too seriously."

18

Difficulty with Transitions

Barrier: When your child is having a great time, sometimes she does not want to stop. Increased behavior problems can occur around times of transition. Attempts to transition her to a less-preferred activity can lead to feelings of upset and meltdowns. When these meltdowns happen at the end of a playdate, it can be embarrassing both for you and for your child.

Coaching Suggestion: Teach your child the word *transition* and make sure she understands that it means to stop doing one thing and move on to another. It can be extremely helpful to use a timer or visual aid to prepare her for a transition:

- Fifteen minutes before an activity ends, let your child know that a transition is coming so she does not become involved in a new project or game;
- Ten minutes prior to ending the activity, give another reminder to start wrapping up whatever she is doing; and,
- When only five minutes remain, give a directive that it is time to put away whatever she is doing and get ready to transition.

In approaching a transition in this way, by the time it is upon her, she has been thinking about it for a while. This works well to prepare your child for the transition and can prevent a meltdown. Using visual timers that allow your child to see the passing of time may also help her understand transitions. Consider using some of the great visual timer apps that are available for smartphones and can be found by doing a quick search.

Another easy transition tool to purchase is an inexpensive analog clock. Use colored window markers in green, yellow and red to draw colored arrows in five-minute intervals to show your child time moving. She can see when she can continue to play, when she needs to start thinking about stopping, and when she needs to actually stop.

You can give your child a sense of control over the transition by asking her how many minutes she needs to wrap up what she is doing. For example, "How many more minutes do you think you need to finish what you are doing? Dinner will be soon." Most kids will offer up a reasonable number of minutes and if not, you might also suggest to your child that she can *freeze* the activity and return to it later.

Before your child goes on a playdate, a trip to the playground, or other fun activity, review with her your expectations for when the activity is over. Review with her what a *polite goodbye* looks and sounds like. Reward her with verbal praise or a small treat in the car when she makes a successful transition.

A change in routine card can also help with transitions. See page 91.

Suggested Social Language:

"In fifteen minutes, we're going to get ready to transition."

"I'm sorry that we only have a few minutes left and that game will take too long. Is there a quicker game that we could play instead?"

"How many more minutes between one and ten do you need to finish?"

"How are we going to make this a polite goodbye today?"

"We have five more yellow minutes on the clock to finish up and then it will be red and time to clean up."

19

Not Understanding Humor

Barrier: Your child may have difficulty understanding humor and/or sarcasm and might frequently interpret what is said in a literal way. He may accuse others of being mean to him or making fun of him when his peers were actually just joking in a friendly manner.

Coaching Suggestion: If your child misunderstands a joke or an intended joke by a peer, you might ask him, "Does his face look serious to you?" or "Does his face match his tone of voice?" and "Do you think he would really say something mean like that to you?"

Provide your child with prepared responses to use if he is not sure if someone is joking, such as, "You must be kidding, right?" or "I think you are just trying to mess with me." You may need to practice these responses so they are delivered in a lighthearted tone of and not too seriously.

Humor is an important part of friendships. If your child has an education plan at school, it may be helpful to add a goal which addresses the use of humor. At home, encourage using humor as a family. Point out when something is meant to be funny or a joke or when you are using sarcasm (in person or, better yet, on a TV show that includes laugh tracks).

Most children who struggle with interpreting humor also have difficulty with understanding figurative language such as idioms and metaphors. It is easy to test your child to see if this is the case just by asking if he knows what one means. An online search can provide various types of card decks or books that you can purchase to practice learning these plays on language.

Suggested Social Language:

"Bodies and faces talk, too."

"Can you tell if this is mean teasing or friendly joking?"

"Do his tone of voice and facial expression match?"

"I'm observing that he is laughing with you, not at you."

20

Poor Self-Modulation

Barrier: Your child may have difficulty controlling the volume of her voice or her excitement level when engaging in a high-energy activity. She may be aware that she gets overly excited, or she may need it brought to her attention.

Coaching Suggestion: When your child is getting really excited, try using *The Incredible 5-Point Scale* by Kari Dunn Burton and Mitzi Curtis. There are various scales in their book that may be used for various scenarios. For example, to modulate voice volume, Dunn Burton and Curtis suggest:

5 = Screaming/emergency only

4 = Recess/outside voice

3 = Classroom voice/talking

2 = Soft voice/whisper

1 = No talking at all

The scales can be used for many different modulation needs such as, silliness, intensity, competitiveness, etc. Introduce your child to the 5-point scales and teach him that a level 3 or 4 is appropriate for playing with other kids. Call to her attention when she is getting beyond a "4" and give her strategies to modulate back down. Deep, slow breaths are the fastest way to start to control the excitement. Taking a short break or getting something cold to drink can also reduce her level of intensity.

Have your child observe how the other kids are acting to determine if she is blending in with the excitement level of those around her. We use the term *social matching*. Specifically point out to her the impact her actions are having on others when she is not matching their excitement level. For example, did she notice the other kids leave the game shortly after it began? It may be helpful to work out some discrete hand signals between you and your child so as not to draw attention to your coaching.

If your child struggles with self-modulation she may need active games explained to her in very concrete terms. For example, explain that when playing tag, the person who is "it" should tag the other player with only one, flat-palmed hand, on the arm or back. This prevents accidental two-handed shoves.

It can be helpful to talk to your child about *levels of fun*:

Level 1 Fun: All is going great. Voice and body are fine.

Level 2 Fun: An adult shows up to intervene.
               Need to lower voice and dial down intensity.

Level 3 Fun: It's dangerous and has to stop.

Suggested Social Language:

"Is your voice sticking out or blending in?"

"Is the level of excitement too much, too little, or just right?"

"Just checking in! What level of fun are you at?"

"Show me how you're going to go from 4 to 2."

"Let's look around. Do you match everyone else?"

Section 2:

A Parent's Role as a Social Coach

As the parent of a child with social challenges, your child needs you to be an integral part of his social life. You can be a social coach for your child and do much to support his friendships. While it takes time and energy to nurture friendships for your child, committing to helping your child make and keep friends is the single most important element for his social success. He needs you to identify, pursue, and schedule social opportunities and then treat those social events with the importance they deserve. Phone a friend, set up a social event, and do not cancel unless it is absolutely necessary. Treat a playdate or a social event as if it is an important appointment.

This section will offer ideas for you to:

- Create social opportunities;

- Prepare for social situations;

- Coach your child through social challenges;

- Approach school systems for help; and,

- Foster social independence.

The first step is to be a social role model and to create a social opportunity.

1

Being a Social Role Model

Your child learns by watching you be a positive social role model. If you do not tend to have friends over to socialize, then your child is not getting the chance to see you interact with your friends. Tap into your own social circle and consider having your friends over, and have them bring their kids, too. You may be a bit social-phobic yourself and feel that you do not have what it takes to entertain people. Here are some tips and easy social event ideas:

He Can Help: Your child can pick up toys, dust and vacuum, fill a cooler with ice, etc. Provide a to-do list for him (and any siblings) so that he knows how he can help get ready for a social event.

Cleaning Your House: Pretty clean is clean enough. If you wait until your house is spotless, you will likely never entertain.

Invite Using E-mail: Save time by using online invitation websites of which there are several to choose from.

Create a Social Schedule: Schedule regular social get-togethers. For example, try meeting friends or family at:

- An apple orchard, pumpkin patch, a working farm;

- A bowling alley; or,

- A movie theatre, etc.

Dinner Clubs: Take turns hosting and making dinner.

Pot Luck Suppers: Everyone brings a dish and shares in the cooking.

Take Out: Take turns buying pizza (and serve it on paper plates for easy clean up).

Game Night: Kids play games together; adults do the same on their own; or everyone plays together. There are many great all-age group games available including Apples to Apples™ and Spot It™.

Make-Your-Own Night: Try a pizza, taco, or sundae night where each family brings an ingredient and everyone makes their own. Another fun thing to try is Cupcake Wars. Bake the cupcakes ahead of time. Make enough cupcakes for each child to decorate two or three cupcakes. Provide candies, sprinkles, licorice, or fruit leather and vanilla frosting with food coloring. Then let the creativity begin!

Develop a Neighborhood Signal: Encourage families in your neighborhood with pools, fire pits, or some other readily available group play setting to create a drive-by signal that indicates an invitation to join them. Good examples of open invitation signals are a flag on the mailbox or a colorful and visible marker at the end of the driveway such as a message written in chalk.

2

If There Is No Friend to Invite

Not having anyone to invite over is a common challenge and, if this is your child's reality at the moment, she is not the only one. Over time, a lack of friends can chip away at your child's self-esteem. You should be persistent in having your child try out new groups and different activities until a connection is made.

Social Groups – These are perfect places to make new friends with social support. Shop around for social groups that are a nice match for your child. Ask to visit in advance of joining to determine if the group meets the developmental and support needs of your child, while also assessing the fun factor. It is our belief that social learning needs to be play-***full.***

Girl/Boy Scouts – You may need to check out several troops to see which one has the best personalities and activities for your child. Consider being the troop leader so that you can set the tone for the group yourself.

Sports – If your child is not skilled or interested in the more popular team sports, consider fencing, archery, swimming, martial arts, wrestling, gymnastics, skateboarding, golf, roller/ice skating, or some other sport where kids practice individual skills in a group setting.

Volunteer – Your child can volunteer at a food pantry, read to younger kids at a day care, walk dogs, help out at animal shelters and nursing homes, partner at Special Olympics, or assist in a group public gardening project.

Parks and Playgrounds – Public play spaces offer a way to meet new friends, even if just for the day.

Online (carefully) – Some gaming sites offer a friend element, like stuffed animals who are cared for online.

These and other video games and websites sometimes include a chat component. You should be aware of who your child is communicating with at all times and provide rules around friending people online. For example, a good rule is to tell your child she can only friend people he knows in real life.

Participate in School Clubs/Activities – Encourage participation in after-school activities. If your child needs a social coach for these activities, hire a high school student to be her social companion for the event. Preferably, you would spend some time guiding the teen coach on the type of support that may be needed. This has been particularly successful for middle school dances!

Join Community Clubs or Create Your Own:

- Book clubs
- Scrapbooking
- Bunco
- Dominoes
- Movie night
- Themed clubs (Star Wars™ or Minecraft™, for example)
- Community service projects
- Safe, online communities or video chatting

Ask Teachers/Guidance Counselors – Ask school staff if there are any kids that they feel might be a good fit as a friend for your child. School may also offer peer buddies, recess clubs, or lunch bunch groups that your child could participate in.

Consider Kids Younger and Older – Your child's friends do not need to be the same age. Very nice friendships can have an age span of four years or even more.

A total lack of friends is an incredibly sad situation. Tell your child who is in this situation to hang in there. There are friends for her out there and she has just not found them yet.

Always watch for signs of depression and get mental health counseling, if needed. Support your child with the message that others will make their choices about who they have as friends. Sometimes there is not much we can do about how other people respond to our interest in a friendship. Remind her there <u>are</u> friends out there for her and she should not give up.

It is important that your child feel good about herself despite the current challenges she is having. Teach your child to be optimistic by reminding her to be and do her personal best each day. In the meantime, observe how she is interacting with others and coach her through his difficulties. Offer to play games or have special time with her so she feels valued. Volunteering can be especially valuable in building and maintaining self-esteem during a search for friendship.

3

Preparing for Playdates, Social Events, and Life Changes

Your child with social challenges may benefit from knowing what to expect in situations (to the extent that we adults know what to expect). The more you can prepare your child by previewing an upcoming social situation, the more adept he will become at handling these events.

Coach Your Child Prior to a Social Event – Remind your child what is expected of him and what he can expect to happen as you are driving to your destination, or some earlier time before the event occurs. Some kids may need to be coached several times before the same event. Be as specific as you can. Telling your child to "be good" is too broad of a statement. Specific expectations may be, "I expect that you will stay near me at the mall, not touch anything in the stores without permission, and use good table manners when we meet our friends at the food court."

Coach Your Child During a Social Event – Discretely coach during the event, as needed. Develop hand signals for common behaviors to remind him how to behave so that he is not embarrassed and you are not repeatedly using his name to re-direct his actions.

Review Social Conduct After a Social Event – Give feedback in a "sandwich" manner to soften any constructive criticism that needs to be communicated to your child. *Sandwiching* means to give praise for what he did really well, and then provide constructive feedback on what may have been done differently, followed by more praise.

Social Scenarios or Stories – Outlining what is likely to happen in a story format can greatly help your child prepare for what to expect. The scenario can be handwritten or drawn, done on computer software such as PowerPoint, or presented in scrapbook or photo album format. Writing a social scenario may be useful for social and life events, such as:

- Holidays
- Vacations
- Outings (a trip to the zoo, or to the beach, for example)
- A new school
- Family member hospitalization or illness
- Medical testing
- Job loss
- Death in the family
- Divorce or separation
- New baby arrival
- Visit to a relative's house
- Major achievements (for example, winning an award)
- Introducing a new pet
- Moving to a new home
- Sibling going away to college
- Grandparent moving in
- Sports competition or championship
- Playdates (at home or at a friend's house)

Reviewing what is likely to happen can be a tremendous tool in alleviating social anxiety. Of course, not everything always goes according to plan so every situation should always be discussed with the caveat, "This is what I expect will happen but it may not be exactly like this." Preparing your child for the possibility of a change may be enough to prevent a meltdown.

4

What to Do When the Friend Arrives

Before a friend arrives at your house for a playdate, coach your child on how to greet the friend and make her feel welcome. Put away any special toys that your child may not want to share. Coach your child on how to introduce siblings, to give a short tour of the house if it is her friend's first visit, and to ask the friend what he or she would like to do first. To encourage independence (and so that kids are not continually asking for ideas about what to do), we suggest having a list of ideas posted somewhere in the house with activities that kids typically enjoy. A sample list might include:

- Color
- Play with play dough
- Play house
- Do puzzles
- Catch bugs
- Play video games
- Play basketball
- Jump on a trampoline
- Do beading (or other craft)
- Race cars
- Play with Legos™ or other building-type toy
- Dance
- Play soccer
- Play badminton
- Play Bocce ball
- Fly a kite
- Ride bikes, scooters, skate boards
- Play a board game
- Have a scavenger hunt
- Create and conquer obstacle courses

5

When Playdates Do Not Go Well

Less than successful playdates can occur for several reasons. When this happens, parents can help by observing the interactions to see what is causing disagreements, problems, or boredom. It may be something that your child is doing to cause his friend to react in a negative way, but it may also be something the friend does, or the way the two of them interact with each other.

If playdates frequently do not go well for your child, try to determine if it happens with a few different kids or just one particular friend. If it happens consistently, then it may be that one or more of the barriers mentioned in Section 1 is making the social interaction difficult. Observe the kids as they play and listen to the discussion between them. Listen for obvious signs of annoyance, including:

"Hey, it was my turn!"
"No fair!"
"Let's play something else."
"Let's do what I want now."
"I told you I'm not good at this."
"Ugh! You're so annoying!"
"Stop doing that."
"Quit it!"
"Cheater."
"You're doing it wrong."
"I told you I was good at this."
"Oh man, you're horrible at this!"
"I'm going to win!"
"You're going to lose!"
"Ugh! I hate this game!"
"I'm bored."
"Are your neighbors home? Maybe we can play there?"
"What time is my mom coming to get me?"

Listen to see if your child is being ignored by his friend, or if the friend is being ignored by your child. If a child is repeatedly trying to get the other child's attention, he may become more aggressive to gain that attention. Even if your child has persistent social challenges, the reason for the conflict may be due to the actions of the friend. In either case, intervention is warranted.

Keeping your demeanor light and inquisitive is the key to social coaching this situation. Say something along the lines of:

"Hey guys, how's it going?" If it's not going well, this question will likely be met with a grumbling, whiny, or at the least an unenthusiastic response.

"Well, that didn't sound too exciting!" you reply with a smile on your face and in your voice. "Maybe it's time to move on to something else that you both like to do." Then offer suggestions that are very different from what they are doing. If they are playing a game where competition is involved, suggest they go for a bike ride. If they have been outside for a long time, suggest a board game. If they have been running around, perhaps they could settle in to a craft activity. If they cannot seem to find something to do, offer some ideas or lead them to the suggestion list posted in the house. For older kids, suggest some active activities such as playing basketball, skateboarding, or taking the dog for a walk. You can also offer ideas for creative outlets such as creating a game or making a video.

If they are really having a tough time, it may be time to whip up some cookie dough or make sundaes. Kids can get cranky if they are hungry and, if treats are allowed, serving them will break the negative spell they are under. If healthy snacks are in order, try to make them fun or let the kids make the snack themselves. While snacking, try to bring the energy level up by helping them start a conversation, suggesting that the kids attempt a tongue twister, or encouraging them to share jokes.

Lengthy playdates can also lead to friendship difficulties. If the kids typically start to have a hard time after being together for a long while, try shortening the playdate by a half hour so that it is more likely to end on a positive note. If the playdate does not end well, lay the groundwork for next time by commenting, "I noticed that you guys had a bit of a rough patch today but I know that you will have a better time next time since you are such good friends."

If your child does something unexpected during the playdate, explain the behavior to the friend. For example, if your child talks to himself a lot and does this while with a friend, explain to your child that his friend may find that confusing. Then ask the friend, "Is it confusing when he talks and you don't know if he's talking to you?" The friend will usually agree when asked directly and this gives you the opportunity to explain, "He does that sometimes. Next time, you could ask him if he's talking to you or just out loud." You could also say something more generic like, "That's something that he is working on handling better so thank you for being such a patient friend."

6

Playdate Reciprocation (or Lack Thereof)

In our society good manners suggest that when we invite someone to our home, the invitation will be reciprocated. Unfortunately that doesn't always happen. Lack of reciprocation for playdates can cause you to wonder about the depth of the friendship. It can be frustrating for you and lead you to think that the friendship is over; however, lack of reciprocation can happen for many different reasons:

Siblings: If your child's friend has siblings, he or she may have someone to play with at home. Scheduling outside playdates may not be as much of a priority for that family as it is for your family.

Busy Parents: The friend's parents may be busy and simply do not think about calling your child to come over for a playdate. They may be preoccupied with their own lives and might be feeling too busy to add your child into their home for the afternoon.

Neighborhood Friends: The friend might be fortunate enough to be able to find friends in his or her own neighborhood. This is far more convenient for the parents than scheduling playdates that require driving.

Fastidiousness: Some people are very particular about the neatness and cleanliness of their homes and do not enjoy having kids running around.

House "Vibe": Some homes have a very relaxed vibe and kids tend to have more fun in that environment. If the playdate is always at your house, that just might be a compliment.

Parent Working From Home: Your child's friend may have parents who work from home and who might be reluctant to have kids over during work hours. They may need the house quiet for phone calls and concentration and cannot be distracted by kids playing, or are unable to watch them as closely as needed due to the attention they must give to their work.

Challenging Behaviors: The other parents may feel uncomfortable if your child has exhibited challenging behaviors on a playdate in the past.

Distance: If the friend is from another town, the commute might be a hindrance to getting the kids together.

Friendships are so critical that, even if the playdates are not being reciprocated, it is vital for you to continue to invite your child's friends over to your house. As long as the kids enjoy spending time together, it is worth the inconvenience that it can cause. However, if it becomes too much, or if the other family is starting to use you as a babysitting service, we suggest the use of this social language:

"Jamie was here last time so it would be great if they could play at your house today."

"Jamie would love to come play with Amanda; she's been asking to play dress-up with Amanda lately."

"No problem. I can have Amanda over here today and we'll plan on your house next time."

Hopefully, these suggestions will result in reciprocation but, if the pattern continues and is making you uncomfortable, you may have to be more direct:

"I've noticed that Jaime hasn't been invited to your house in quite some time. Did she misbehave during prior visits? I want to help her understand if she was inappropriate in any way."

7

When Your Child Is Excluded

Being excluded or shunned is a very painful experience for your child and for you. It is important for you to try to analyze why this might be happening and intervene, if necessary. That said, it may not be anything your child did or didn't do that caused him to be excluded, but simply due to another child having had a mean moment.

Your child may find the social pressure of one-to-one interaction to be intimidating. Having a group dynamic might be easier for him. Or, he may be a child that finds a group overwhelming. To minimize the chance of exclusion, have either only two kids play together, or four or more. A group of three kids usually ends up with two of the kids teaming up in some way while excluding the third child. It is fairly common for a triangle of kids to not get along while playing. If two of the three are best friends, or siblings, their connection can make the third child in the trio feel excluded or even bullied.

Remind all the kids that everyone needs to be included in a game or activity before any excluding has happened. It also helps to stay aware for the more subtle ways that kids can be excluded. For example, you might notice two kids making silly jokes and laughing but stop laughing when your child tries his own joke. A reminder to be fair and give everyone's joke a chance is probably enough.

If your child feels excluded or has a difficult time joining in a group, teach him to say, "I'd like to play with you. Tell me what you are doing." This is very different from what kids typically say, which is "Can I play with you?" A yes or no question makes it easy for other kids to say no, but, "Tell me what you are doing" helps your child to conform to what a group is already playing. Your child may be excluded because, when he does join a group, he tries to take over the interaction, or he may change or complicate the game or activity.

A very typical form of exclusion is when kids create clubs and gangs at recess. This is very painful for the child being excluded and should be addressed by school personnel. When recess aides take note of exclusionary games, and address the issue with the kids, they will be less likely to continue to exclude. When kids become aware that adults are watching, mean behavior and bullying are less likely to occur. Many adults do not know how to intervene. Any adult who is aware of exclusionary play by kids should say, "Look, I see what's happening here. I don't like it and I want it to stop. I'll be checking in to make sure that everyone is being included." The adult should always follow up so the kids know that he or she really will check in as promised.

A more subtle form of exclusion, but a very common one, is flip flop friends. These are kids who will play with your child when there is no one else around, have nothing else to do, or to gain access to your child's belongings (a toy, a video game system, etc.). They will then turn around and ignore your child at the bus stop or at recess, or when another friend is available to play.

Flip flop friends can be very troublesome for your child. If he wants friends very badly he might tolerate this type of behavior in order to have one. It may help for your child to call it out by saying something like, "Look, are we friends or not? I don't like being treated this way." It may also help your child to go through our Real Friends Checklist to see whether or not the relationship is one he wants to continue pursuing and or whether the relationship is genuine.

Real Friends Checklist

- ✓ Hangs out with you when not in school;

- ✓ Texts or calls you regularly;

- ✓ Is trustworthy with your secrets;

- ✓ Makes you feel good about who you are;

- ✓ Does not try to change you or make you feel less than;

- ✓ Listens;

- ✓ Is honest and respectful; and,

- ✓ Likes you for you.

8

When Other Kids Take Advantage of Your Child's Special Needs

It is normal to feel a great deal of anger in situations where other children are taking advantage of your child due to her special needs. An example is when your child with special needs is "It" in a game of hide and seek, and other kids leave their hiding spots to run to other places in order to confuse your child. It is important to stay calm when addressing this type of behavior, and to provide re-direction rather than anger.

Bring it to the attention of the kids so that *they* know that *you* know what they are doing. Try saying, "Hey guys, I noticed that when Susie is 'It,' not all of you are staying in your hiding place. Remember to be fair with everyone and play by the rules." If it happens persistently, you could suggest another game and make it clear that you did not like the way they were playing the earlier game. Clear language to use is, "I see what is going on and I want it to stop."

Asking questions is another strategy to try with kids. For example, you could ask, "Is there some reason why everyone is laughing except Susie?" If you sense that something nasty is going on, try, "Why do I have a bad feeling about this game you are playing? Is something going on?" Mentioning it will likely make it stop because the kids know you are aware of the behavior.

9

Getting Details About Your Child's Social Life

You might feel frustrated by the lack of information you get about your child's social and school life. Typically the answer to "How was your day?" is "Fine." This exchange does not give you much information about what went on while your child was at school. There are ways to ask that can help you, as a parent, get more of a feel for your child's social life at school. To assess the situation, try:

Best part of the day, worst part of the day: During dinner time, ask each person to share one thing that was the best part of their day and one thing that was the worst part. This provides an opportunity for everyone to share some details about everyone else's lives while also teaching your child to listen to others.

Ask more specific questions about his day (just be sure to not ask all at once or it will seem like an interrogation):

- Who are the really nice kids in school?
- Are there any kids who aren't nice?
- Who did you play with at recess?
- What did you do at recess?
- Who did you sit with on the bus? At lunch?
- What do the kids chat about during lunch and recess?
- Does anyone get bullied?
- Has anyone called you a bully?
- Is there any other drama at school?

Talk to your child's teacher:

- Contact your child's teacher and ask if he has friends at school. Ask if the teacher can connect you with their parents so you can set up playdates. If the teacher cannot disclose this information due to privacy issues, you can give permission for the teacher to share your contact information. If the teacher does not see friendships forming, ask if he or she has ideas as to why. Some teachers are reluctant to share this type of information because parents can become defensive. Because understanding the issues is an important step in being able to provide support for friendships, it is key that the teacher feels he or she can be honest with you. Your child may act very differently at school than he does at home and you may not be aware of the barriers that are hindering social connections.

- Ask if he or she has suggestions for who to invite for a playdate.

- Ask if there are parent volunteer opportunities for you to help out in the classroom. You will be able to view the dynamics of the social environment for yourself.

If possible, volunteer during recess and get to know the recess aides. If you become friendly with the aides, they may keep a closer eye on your child and contact you if they are seeing issues. Recess aides can be a valuable resource, especially if they see that you support their efforts and are open to their feedback.

You could also discuss your child's socialization with the guidance counselor or school psychologist. It may be helpful to ask him or her to observe your child's socialization during lunch and recess. He or she can give you feedback and perhaps provide support for your child.

10

Helping Your Child Read Social Cues

Your child may not pick up on social cues from other kids no matter how obvious the cues may be to others. If your child has this difficulty she will need social skills explicitly taught to her. You may need to point out cues she is missing that you think are obvious. This is certainly true if your child has a diagnosis of a social communication disorder such as Autism Spectrum Disorder (ASD) or Non-Verbal Learning Disability (NLD). On the other hand, your child may also be one of those children without a diagnosis who needs to be educated on how to interact. She may not be a child that picks up on social information and feedback naturally. She will need to understand the impact that she has on others and how to adjust her actions if those actions are unpleasant to others.

To some extent, she will need to learn how to conform. Kids can, and should, be taught social blending. This is not an attempt to discount their uniqueness in any way. Some adults become uncomfortable when we talk about conformity, but a level of conformity is expected by our society. As an example, if, in the middle of a meeting at work, you decided to jump up on the table and cluck like a chicken, you would lose credibility with your co-workers. They will certainly be talking about you behind your back the rest of the day. Your child may not do things that seem as dramatic as that example, but she may say and do things that are socially inappropriate for given situations.

To address this important skill, coach your child to:

- Take a step back and look around to see what everyone else is doing and try to match it as long as it is not dangerous or destructive behavior;

- Consider whether or not she is currently sticking out or blending in with the group; and,

- Evaluate whether or not her actions are creating *uncomfortable thoughts* in other people's minds.

Your child may not realize the aspects of her interactions that are making friendships challenging. With patience and time, you can teach your child to evaluate her demeanor and adjust as necessary. Just as you have learned to adjust to different social situations and environments (remember, you wouldn't wear an evening gown or a tuxedo to a casual barbecue), your child can learn about social norms and blending in.

11

When Your Child Does Not Talk Much

Social conversation can be very difficult for your child with social challenges. Lack of conversation skills may be due to anxiety, uncommon or few interests, or shyness. To foster conversation skills, some ideas to suggest to your child are:

- Think of events that have recently occurred;
- Think of events that are happening soon;
- Use chat rings or card packs to provide conversation starters;
- Ask about the other person's interests;
- Ask about the other person's favorites;
- Play a board game that encourages conversation (such as Headbanz™ or Apple to Apples™); or,
- Make observations about what is going on around him.

For your child who is reluctant to talk to others due to social anxiety, as mentioned in a previous section, *Growing Up Brave* by Donna Pincus is a good resource. Ms. Pincus's book addresses this critical topic from many angles and provides concrete strategies to help children with anxiety. Her CD, *I Can Relax,* is also a useful tool to help children learn to manage stress and anxiety with relaxation techniques.

It is also important to consider that your own childhood friendship experiences may differ from your child's friendships. Some friendships rely more on a quiet understanding rather than lengthy conversation. As long as kids are enjoying each other's company, intervention is generally not necessary.

12

Sleepovers: A Test of Independence

Whether or not to allow your child to go on a sleepover at a friend's house is a personal family decision. As a parent, you need to feel comfortable that your child will be safe when spending the night with a friend. Factors to consider are familiarity with the family; comfort level with older siblings and their friends; pets; cleanliness; and family values.

The first time she's invited to spend the night at another home, she will be both excited and anxious about being away from home overnight. She may worry that she will wake up and want to come home. Before she goes, discuss a game plan with her and the host family, if that should that occur. Tell her that it's okay if she calls you and asks to come home. Should that occur, go ahead and bring her home, and let her try again another time. Forcing her to stay could upset her further and make her more anxious about trying it again. It might be helpful to start with a half sleepover (also known as sleep-under) to experience the fun of a sleepover and staying up late. She would still arrive at her friend's house with a sleeping bag and pajamas but would plan to be picked up to go home before going to bed.

As long as your child is safe staying with the other family, a sleepover can be an important rite of passage. It gives your child the opportunity to break away from the family temporarily and allows her a little independence. She will also practice different social skills in this setting. Many times kids show their best selves to others.

Before the sleepover, it would be helpful if you could:

Dinner/Breakfast – Coach her through what to do if she does not like what is being served and how to ask for seconds. Review her table manners before she goes. Remind her to bring dishes to the sink when dinner is over.

Basic table manners –

- Napkin on the lap
- Fork and knife should be placed on the plate when not in use and not on the placemat
- Use napkin frequently
- No elbows on the table
- No talking while chewing food
- Take small bites
- Compliment the cook
- Wait to start eating until everyone is sitting, unless the host tells you it is okay to begin eating
- Always say please and thank you

Before bed – Explain to her that she should wash her face and brush her teeth just like she would at home. Coach her to know that, if she is not given a towel, she will have to politely ask for one.

Prepare her to compromise – Make her aware that she may need to compromise on bedtime routines when on a sleepover. Light levels, music or no music, door opened or closed, are some of the things that may be different during a sleepover. She should be prepared with strategies to handle these differences or family rules that may be different from her own.

Sleeping arrangements – Explain that she may have to sleep on the floor in a sleeping bag. Before agreeing to a sleepover, she may need the maturity to be able to sleep on a hard floor without complaining to her host.

Waking during the night – Plan ahead of time and prepare your child with what to do if she cannot fall asleep or if she wakes up and feels scared. Should she wake her friend? Call home? Wake the friend's parents? Decide on a plan of action so she is prepared for what to do and make the hosting parent aware of the plan.

Waking up – Remind her that, when she wakes up, she should pack up her things and willingly have whatever breakfast is being served.

Special dietary needs – If your child has special dietary needs, these should be reviewed with the hosting family prior to the sleepover. Send your child with special foods so she knows she has something safe to eat. Remind her that the special food is only if she cannot eat what the family is serving and not permission to eat double of everything. She should bring enough to share since the friend may also enjoy her special food.

If she has not been invited to a sleepover by the time she is in 5th grade (or thereabouts), consider hosting one at your house.

13

Approaching School Systems

Schools can help with social skills in numerous ways. Getting along with others is a critical life skill and necessary to function successfully in society. Good social skills improve academic performance by helping children participate in group discussions, work on projects together, respect the opinions of others, and eventually obtain employment and financial independence. It is critical that all kids feel connected to the school community.

Most schools have personnel or a department that addresses the social/emotional needs of students. The term used for this role can vary and you may have one or more of these titles in your school system, including:

- Guidance Counselor
- School Adjustment Counselor
- Social Worker
- Liaison
- School Psychologist
- Speech-Language Pathologist

We will generically use the term guidance counselor to refer to all of these staff members.

Although guidance counselors are responsible for the social and emotional well-being of all children in the school, they generally work with kids who have been referred by other educators or parents who have requested support. Their time is usually in high demand and they may not necessarily know if your child is having social difficulty unless you call them or meet to discuss your concerns. Once informed, they can be immensely helpful.

Guidance counselors can provide:

- Lunch bunch groups
- Recess clubs
- Girls/boys groups
- Role-playing scenarios
- Whole class discussions
- Videos that demonstrate role-modeling
- Counseling and advice

Guidance counselors are also able to:

- Connect children with similar profiles from other schools in town
- Form mentoring groups with older kids or peers
- Organize self-esteem building connections (for example, have an older child help a younger child in school)
- Create "pal" programs
- Observe unstructured time, like recess, and provide advice
- Provide counseling and/or simply a comfortable environment
- Help children understand each other
- Practice conversation skills

Recess clubs are a concept that is becoming more popular in school systems as a way to help students access recess. A recess club offers an adult-guided activity that is available during recess. For example, the guidance counselor may facilitate a kick ball game or offer friendship bracelet instruction during recess. Usually the children who need it most drive the theme of the recess club. In fact, most recess clubs are driven by an individual child's education plan. The participants in the recess club are completely unaware that the club was formed to support a particular child. The kids still experience recess but there is an adult who is facilitating the activity and providing social coaching, as needed. It is a great way to offer a safe activity for a child who cannot find an accepting friend group and who may wander around the playground without playing with anyone. A guidance counselor, speech-language pathologist, teacher, recess aide, or parent volunteer can facilitate the club.

If your child has a diagnosed disability and has an education plan, the guidance counselor can be asked to attend team meetings and assist in creating social goals for your child. Potential goal topics include:

- Use of unstructured time
- Active listening skills
- Conflict resolution
- Conversation skills
- Understanding idioms and sarcasm
- Anger and frustration management
- Impulsiveness
- Shyness
- Sensory integration dysfunction
- General awkwardness
- Social, verbal, and physical communication
- Non-verbal language
- Modulation of voice and behavior
- Personal space
- Perseveration
- Bullying prevention
- Cliques and mean comments
- Identifying and managing feelings

For your child with a diagnosed disability, we suggest that he have a social goal in his education plan each year. Appropriate social goals depend on the age of your child, and may include:

Preschool – Teach interactive play skills, sharing, turn taking, and how to ask to play. Introduce elimination games such as tag or musical chairs.

Kindergarten – Third Grade - Access recess; teach jump rope songs or the rules for four square, or whatever popular games are being played by peers. Include strategies for how to handle a situation when kids do not play fairly (for example, review the rules, use "I-based language").

Fourth – Fifth Grade - Prepare your child with strategies for how to handle a situation when social language is confusing for him. Learn idioms so that he understands not to take those phrases literally.

Middle School (Sixth – Eighth Grade) – How to defend and/or deflect negativity, managing strong feelings, self-esteem and empowerment, blending in to the social culture, online social media safety, and texting.

High School – Blending in to the social culture; managing strong feelings; self-esteem and empowerment; online social media safety; texting, dating and relationships; and social skills needed for educational opportunities post high school and employment.

For all grades, bullying prevention should be taught. Some state anti-bullying laws require that education plans explicitly teach children who have been diagnosed with Autism Spectrum Disorders about bullying. This is so they can understand if they are being bullied and take steps to make it stop.

Bullying is a formidable social topic all by itself (and one we plan to address in a future book). To address the issue of bullying in schools, we have developed the How to

Make & Keep Friends Bullying Prevention initiative. Our program:

- provides practical, actionable tips and strategies to create a positive school culture;
- transforms the way children interact with each other;
- teaches students social coping skills for the most common problems;
- implements a framework;
- gets the entire school community on the "same page;" and,
- creates a positive chain reaction of respect.

The program we have created coaches kids on how to improve their confidence, social skills, and language. More information on this program can be found on our website at www.HowToMakeAndKeepFriends.com.

14

Anticipating Social Triggers

As her parent, you probably have learned to predict when your child is going to become anxious, overwhelmed, and/or frustrated. When your child is experiencing one or all of these emotions, she may react in socially inappropriate ways.

Whenever possible, inform your child of what is expected to happen and, if necessary, accommodate her needs in order to reduce anxiety and maladaptive reactions. For example, school assemblies can be exciting and fun, but they also disrupt the expected flow of the day. It can become quite loud as kids settle in to an auditorium or gym. Informing your child of the assembly ahead of time, so she has an opportunity to process the change, can help. We suggest having a sensory-sensitive child enter the assembly just before it starts, to avoid exposure to the noises associated with the whole school congregating together. This can make the difference between your child being able to enjoy the special event and your child experiencing sensory overload before the event even starts.

Other environments that may prove challenging are:

- Movie theaters
- Amusement parks
- Field trips
- Parties
- Playdates

We recommend using a change of routine card when the schedule differs from the norm. The card can simply state:

The new _____ is _____.

If this worries you:

1. Tell yourself it's OK.

2. Breathe slowly and deeply.

3. Tell yourself you are strong and powerful.

4. Try _____.

(Fill in your own idea)

Example:

The new routine today is a school assembly and it might be loud.

If this worries you:

1. Tell yourself it's OK.

2. Breathe slowly and deeply.

3. Tell yourself you are strong and powerful.

4. Get there early so you can find a quieter spot or one near the door in case you need to ask for a break.

15

Perspective Taking

Your child may be having difficulty making and keeping friends because he may be thinking only about his own needs and wants. He may be having a hard time considering another person's point of view or perspective. Approach teaching this complex social process by asking your child questions that are designed to help him observe what is going on around him, interpret how his actions are impacting others, and learn to see someone else's perspective. By teaching your child social skills with this approach, the goal is that he will eventually be able to analyze his own environment and not need to depend on your social coaching. Three examples:

Child: "It's my room and my stuff."
Parent: **"**Yes it is, but how can you help your friend feel welcome in your room?"

Child: "I'm the guest, so I should get what I want."
Parent: "Can you tell me a way you can fairly decide what to do first?"

Child: "Ben won't play with me."
Parent: "What happened just before he stopped playing with you? Is there something that could have been done or said differently?"

Frequently encourage your child to observe the reactions, responses, and feedback he is receiving from peers. Ideally, you want him to tune in to the impact that his thoughts and actions have on his relationships. Ask him, "Is that a friendly thing to do?" or "Can you guess what your friend is thinking right now?" Check in often and ask, "Is everything okay in here?" Be genuinely enthusiastic when it is. Tell them, "I noticed that you two are playing fairly and getting along great!"

Tone of voice - Your child may have difficulty regulating the tone of his voice and may sound annoyed or harsh when he speaks to others. Sometimes it may be that he is not annoyed and it just sounds as though he is. Or he may be annoyed and not know how, or not realize that he should, mask that annoyance with others. Kids who exhibit very high intelligence can easily become impatient or condescending with peers. Be sure that you bring it to the attention of your child when he is using a less-than-friendly tone. Use the phrase, "I noticed that your tone-of-voice sounds less than friendly. Is there another way that could be said?"

Respect differences – Coach your child that the single best way to show you want to be friends with someone is to ask about things that the other person likes. It is also important that your child understand that other people might enjoy different activities and topics than he does. Your child needs to be taught not to put down someone else's interests or favorite things just because they are not the same as his. Teach him to use the words "in my opinion." For example, your child can learn to say, "In my opinion, I'm not a fan of that TV show. Do you watch (name of another TV show)?" You should also encourage him to try what his friend wants to do, even if he is not interested. Explain to him that doing less-preferred activities with a friend is an important part of friendship.

16

The Value of a Heart-to-Heart Chat

It can be beneficial to your child if you help her understand the big picture of socialization. Social skills do not come easily and it can be a lot of hard work to learn the nuances of how to be friends with others. She may wonder why she has to learn all this stuff. It is so much easier to just do what she does naturally. However, if she understands the big picture implications, she may be more open to social coaching.

If you decide to enroll your child in a social group, you might wonder, "What do I tell my child about why she is going to a social group?" You might describe the social group as another type of after school activity. Your child is probably aware that she experiences social difficulties. You may choose to tell your child that she will be working with a friendship coach or tutor, playing with other kids and having fun while learning and practicing friendship skills.

For example, your child may have a very hard time initiating or maintaining a conversation. If it does not come naturally, then she may not see the point in conversing with others. It helps to explain to her that, when we talk to other people, they learn about us and we learn about them. It shows reciprocity and that we care about their lives and it helps us to become closer friends. This concept may be obvious to us as adults but this is a novel idea to kids with social challenges.

If your child becomes tired and irritated by social coaching, she may need a heart-to-heart chat. When you want your child to really listen, say, "I'm concerned about something and I would like to discuss it with you." This approach will usually get her undivided attention. The conversation could go like this:

Parent: "I'm concerned about something and I would like to discuss it with you. I feel like you're getting frustrated when I try to help you with friendships."

Child: "I am frustrated. I hate that stuff!"

Parent: "I know. I totally get it. This friendship stuff can be kind of confusing."

Child: "I'm not confused. I just don't like it!"

Parent: "How about if I explain why we work on friendship skills?"

Child: "OK (likely grumbled)."

Parent: "I want you to have fun with other kids. I want you to feel comfortable playing with other kids and I want you to be invited to parties. I know this stuff is really hard but friends can be fun. I want that for you. Do you want it too?"

Child: "I guess so."

Parent: "OK, so if we both want that for you, should I keep on trying to help or would you like me to stop?"

Child: "Help me, I guess."

Parent: "Great! I'll keep helping then. How about you try not to get frustrated with me? We can always take a break and talk if you are having a hard time with something I'm doing or saying. How does that sound?"

Child: "OK."

17

Creating a Serene Home Environment

A lack of social skills can make daily life a struggle. Your child needs a home environment that is supportive and allows the struggles of the day to be left behind. Home should a safe place to re-group. This includes monitoring sibling interactions and rivalry.

Families are social environments, too. Good social skills are just as important at home as they are in public. If you find that siblings are fighting with each other, make sure you include your child's siblings in learning the social language and strategies discussed in this book.

As a parent, you are not immune to feeling frustrated, sad, disappointed, or anxious. When you see your child having difficulty, you want to fix it right away. You may worry what his lack of interpersonal skills may mean for his future. If you are experiencing these feelings, take care of yourself, and seek counseling if needed. You want to prevent any negative feelings from being passed on to your child. Sometimes just tapping into your own friendships, and venting out these feelings to another parent or professional, may be the answer.

It is important for you to express to your child that he is a good person and that you like spending time with him. Tell him you are proud of him and that you feel lucky to be his parent. He needs to know that, even if he is temporarily low on friends, he is loved and valued by his family.

18

Achieving Social Independence

Your social support can do much to teach your child how to interact better with others but, at some point, you want him to be able to wean off the social coaching and achieve a level of independent social competence.

Just as math skills can be learned, so too can social skills. With the right tutoring, your child can master the skills he needs to navigate social interactions in all environments.

Look for the moments when your child is demonstrating mastery of a skill. Help him, if needed, and praise him for trying. Listen for your child using, "How about we?" with a friend and problem-solving how to share something without your guidance. Your child may even come and tell you about something that he solved on his own. This occurs frequently with the children we coach. Reward those successes with verbal praise, or create a reward system to positively reinforce when he is getting it right. Going out for a special treat is nice, too! Any trial-and-error attempts that your child makes are the stepping-stones that lead to social success.

It's important to teach kids to think for themselves, observe their surroundings, and determine the impact that they are having on others.

Examples of teaching independence are:

Example 1:

Child: "It's my room and my stuff."
Parent: "Yes, but how can we help your friend feel welcome in your room?"

Example 2:

Child: "I'm the guest, so I get what I want."
Parent: "How can you decide together what to do first? How about rock, paper, scissors?"

Other examples of coaching language:

Parent: "Is that a friendly thing to do?" or "Is that a friendly voice?"

Parent: "You were playing with Herman, but now he's on the other side of the room looking unhappy. Do you know why?"

19

Never Give Up

All children are capable of improving their social skills. Your child may not achieve the highest levels of popularity but we firmly believe that every child has the potential to make one or two good friends. It is just a matter of time before your child finds a friend. As a parent, you have to do everything in your power to create social opportunities and support your child when she is trying to make and keep new friends. As social coaches, we have the extreme gratification of watching true friendships form. When it happens, it is absolutely magical.

If you are a member of the special needs community, it is important to be particularly vigilant of anyone who is enabling poor social skills in your child, or any child. We have heard comments such as, "It's okay, and it's only Cindy. She was having fun! She didn't hit me *that* hard." When people let your child with special needs get away with inappropriate behavior, make light of it, or think it is funny, it is actually being disrespectful of your child with challenges. If it is not appropriate for any child, then it is not appropriate for **all** children. Expectations should not be lowered for your child with special needs. It is important to communicate this in school as well. Provide the guidance department with specific examples to prevent this type of enabling.

You may blame yourself for your child's social challenges. We all do our best as parents and we all make mistakes. Social awkwardness is not anyone's fault and spending energy on this type of thinking does not make things better for your child. That energy is better spent planning get-togethers and social coaching your child on what it takes to be a good friend and help her achieve social success.

Section 3:
Key Phrases & Coaching Examples

For over twelve years, we have coached many children towards increased social success. We have heard the word *magic* used to describe children being able to generalize their social successes in our social groups to school, home, and community as they learn the social language and tips we are sharing with you in this book.

A key element of the magic is partnering with your child to help things go right, rather than a punitive approach when things go wrong. Another aspect is patience with the social learning process. This is not an overnight fix, but your child does have the ability to improve his social skills over time and with support.

When coaching your child, it is important to ask, "What do you think you should do?" or "What do you think would be a good thing to say or try?" If your child cannot come up with the answer, it is important that phrases be scripted for him or that he be given suggestions for what to say. These phrases and suggestions provide him with a social script. With practice, there will come a time when he can create the right social solution on his own.

By providing your child with the consistent and simple social phrases in this section, you will provide him the language he needs to navigate social situations. These phrases should be easy to remember; are meant to be quickly implemented anywhere; and lend themselves to generalization in all environments.

Many of these phrases are included in the first two sections of this book. We have put them here as a quick reference when you are in need of language for a specific situation. We consider these phrases the secret sauce to our social coaching success with kids and are happy to share the recipe and that magic with you!

1

Social Awareness of Others

Phrase: People Need to Feel Special

Your child with social difficulties may lack an awareness of others or be overly-involved in his own interests. This verbiage is helpful:

- When he has difficulty remembering to give proper greetings and goodbyes;

- If he tends to rush into a room or an activity and, in his haste, forgets to acknowledge others;

- When coaching him to remember that it is important to acknowledge other people; and,

- For reinforcing the social expectation of other people of a polite greeting and farewell.

Coaching Example

Let's go over what to do when we get to your friend's house to make him feel special and glad that he invited you for a playdate.

2

Collaborating and Sharing Ideas

Phrase: How About We?

If your child struggles with wanting to control interactions or play with others, she will benefit greatly from learning more collaborative ways of interacting. This phrase will help your child when:

- She is sounding bossy or demanding in her peer interactions;

- She is using the words "You have to . . .," "You need to . . .," "No, you can't do it that way," or "You're doing it wrong," when she is playing with friends;

- She is struggling **when her peers** are being bossy or demanding and she does not know what to do or say; and,

- She doesn't allow everyone to share ideas about how to play or what to do.

Coaching Examples

It looks as though you guys are having a hard time listening to each other's ideas on setting up that dollhouse.

I bet if you both start saying, "How about we try it this way?" or "How about we put it there?" you will both be able to share your ideas better and this will be more fun.

3

Preventing Exclusion

Phrase: I'd Like to Play with You

Think about how many times you hear your child say, "Can I play with you?" Coaching your child to change this language to "I'd like to play with you" does the following:

- Prevents asking a yes or no question that leaves your child open to more easily being rejected or excluded;

- Decreases the chance of other children saying no because they are not given that option and would have to go further out of their way to exclude your child; and,

- Helps your child more smoothly join in.

Follow up by coaching your child to ask the other children in the group to explain what they are doing, or what the rules of the game are, rather than just barging in and impulsively doing something that will upset the other players.

Coaching Example

I can see that you are interested in what the other kids are playing over there. I would like you to go over and say, "I'd like to play, too. What are you doing?"

4

How to Respectfully Disagree

Phrase: In My Opinion

Your child may inadvertently put other people's ideas down or make other people feel badly about something they like if she does not agree or does not like the same things. This phrase is useful for:

- Teaching your child who tends to think that her opinion or idea is the right one, or the only one. This phrase can help her learn that it is okay for others to have a different opinion; and,

- Coaching a child on how to respectfully disagree with someone without demeaning other people for what they like or think.

Coaching Examples

I noticed that you don't seem to like the singer that your friend is talking about [or the television show that she is watching]. Instead of telling her that you don't like the music [or the show], how about you say, "In my opinion, I'm not a fan of _____, but it's okay that you really like his music," or "In my opinion, it's not a show that I like, but it sounds like it's a favorite of yours."

That is much better than hurting your friend's feeling when you say, "I can't believe you like that guy's music…it's just awful!" or "I can't believe you watch that show, it's for babies!"

5

Personal Space

Phrases: I Don't See Any Daylight and
The Invisible Square

Your child may have difficulty recognizing and responding to the personal space requirements of others. These phrases are a way of giving him the message that he needs to:

- Notice if people are leaning back or moving away;

- Recognize how each person has a circle or an invisible fence around him or her about the size of a hula hoop. Some people's circles are larger than others;

- For desk work or table projects, recognize that each person has a space in front of him or her that he should not reach into without asking permission first; and,

- Stay approximately an arm's length away while standing, and a forearm's length away while sitting, to provide enough space for other people.

Coaching Examples

I noticed something that your friend is doing right now. He is sliding away from you. Do you see it too? What do you think you should do?

I know you want that magic marker, but it's in your friend's invisible square. Did you remember to get his permission first?

6

Listening Skills

Phrases: Fronts are Friendly and
I Need Your Brain Right Now

Your child may have trouble staying still, or appearing connected enough to listen to and converse with a peer. These phrases are helpful when your child is:

- Having difficulty with eye contact. Encourage your child to show she is engaged or listening by keeping her shoulders or front turned toward the person who is speaking with her;

- Engaging in parallel play near another child and has her back turned to the peer. By encouraging a friendly "front" you can help your child begin to interact; and,

- Struggling with distraction or such a busy brain that it is hard for her to recognize or respond when someone is trying to tell her something.

Coaching Examples

I noticed that you are playing with the dolls right next to your friend but your back is facing him. Fronts are a lot friendlier, so I'd like to see you turn around so that you will have more fun.

I need your brain right now to tell you something. How do I know I have it? Right, when our eyes or fronts are connected.

7

Reading and Responding to Body Language

Phrase: What is My Face or My Body Saying?

Research suggests that 60-70% of communication is non-verbal. This can cause many friendship struggles for your child who misses non-verbal social cues. Asking him to read a face or body can:

- Help him cue in to non-verbal language by bringing it to his attention; and

- Encourage practicing the interpretation of what other children and people are saying without words.

Rick Lavoie, author of *It's So Much Work to be Your Friend,* suggests watching TV with the sound turned off and asking your child to tell you what he thinks the characters are feeling or thinking. This can increase your child's ability to read non-verbal language.

Coaching Examples

Let's look at your friend's body. Is he enjoying what is happening when you do that?

I'd like you to read my face and tell me what I might be thinking right now.

8

Minding Your Own Business

Phrase: *Is This Observing or Interfering?*

Your child may have difficulty in minding her own business or staying out of situations where her help has not been requested. Helping your child understand the difference between observing and interfering in social interactions assists her with:

- Resisting the urge to tell people how to play a game or to interfere in a game that other people are playing;

- Learning not to "help" in a game or situation if help has not been requested; and,

- Asking others if they would like some help first, before assuming or jumping in with help, advice or explanations of the rules of the game;

- Understanding that observing is done with her eyes and interfering is done with her mouth or hands.

Coaching Example

I can hear that you are trying to help the other kids with their chess game and they are starting to sound upset. Did they ask for help? Is that observing or interfering? What should you do differently?

9

Conversation Skills

> **Phrase: Let's Find a Topic Switching Statement or a Finishing Sentence**

If your child experiences trouble with staying on topic or switching gears, he can leave his listener confused. Sometimes he might stay on a topic long after his listener has lost interest. Coaching him to use a "topic switcher" or "finishing sentence" will benefit your child by:

- Helping him see that a topic is worn out and guiding him towards another conversation idea;

- Providing him a way to "link" his thoughts with phrases such as, "on a different topic" or "that made me think of" or "I need to tell you something before I forget;"

- Creating pauses in a conversation to provide the other person an opportunity to speak; and,

- Teaching him the difference between talking about something because he wants to tell it or because he thinks the other person wants to hear it.

Coaching Examples

I think your friend got confused when you started talking about the dog because you were just talking about video games. Try, "Hey, I want to mention something about my dog before I forget."

I haven't watched much of that TV show. Can we switch to another topic to talk about?

10

When Others Do Not Follow the Rules

Phrase: Who Owns the Problem?

It may be a source of anxiety for your child when other kids are not following the prescribed rules. She might take the problem as her own and can find herself in trouble with his peers for acting like the rule police. Asking your child "who owns this problem?" helps her with:

- Realizing that as long as she is doing what she is supposed to be doing, she does not need to worry about whether the other kids are following the rules; and,

- Learning that it is important to allow the people who are having the problem to solve it themselves.

Coaching Example

I know that the other girl isn't getting in line like she is supposed to…who owns that problem? The teacher? Right. Are you doing what you are supposed to be doing? Great! You have nothing to worry about.

11

Matching Reactions to the Situation

Phrase: Is it a Big Deal or Little Deal?

Your child may need help gauging the size of his reactions to the size of the problem he is experiencing. This phrase helps with:

- Learning to assess a situation or a problem;

- Deciding where a problem rates on a scale of 1 to 10:

  > 8-10: It's an emergency, call for help right away (for example, your friend fell off the jungle gym and isn't getting up);

  > 4-7: It's not an emergency, but I'm not sure what to do so I should ask for help (for example, your friend fell off the jungle gym, got up but is limping);

  > 1-3: I may not like it, but I can deal with what's happening (for example, your friend won't give you a turn on the jungle gym); and then

- Matching the size of his reaction to the size of the problem.

Coaching Example

I know that you are really upset that your friend didn't want to play the same game that you wanted to play. On our problem scale, what number do you think that is? What can you do?

12

Age Inappropriate or
Strange Public Behaviors

Phrase: Creating Uncomfortable Thoughts

Your child may exhibit behaviors that can cause other people to have unwanted thoughts, or uncomfortable thoughts, about her. This phrase often has a powerful impact on a child's behavior and is helpful to:

- Assist your child in conforming to social expectations and the unspoken social norm in our culture; and,

- Bring attention to the reason that other people are reacting to her in the way that they are;

- You can say, "Most kids your age aren't doing that and it's causing you to stick out and creating uncomfortable thoughts about what you are doing."

Coaching Example

I think that you might be bored and I can help you find something to do, but rolling around on the floor is causing some uncomfortable thoughts in the rest of the group. Most kids who are 12 years old don't do that anymore.

13

Meeting Social Expectations

Phrase: Sticking Out or Blending In?

As mentioned in our "Uncomfortable Thoughts" section, our culture has social expectations of all of us, and we all have to conform on some level in our daily lives and interactions. Asking him if he is currently sticking out or blending can help your child:

- Learn to modulate his voice and body. If your child's voice is the only one you can hear during a social activity, then he is sticking out;

- Escape from being teased or bullied. If your child wears his super hero cape to school every day in the 5th grade, he is sticking out and will very likely be teased by his peers;

- Adjust what he is doing or saying to blend in to the social expectations of the current environment; and,

- Prepare for the negative social feedback he might receive if he does make the informed choice to stick out.

Coaching Example
I know that you still really enjoy Thomas the Train. Talking about that in middle school might cause you to stick out and the other kids to be mean and tease you about it. If someone asks, you might just say that you like trains instead of Thomas specifically.

14

Needing to Be Right

Phrase: Was That a Necessary Correction?

Your child might be one that we fondly refer to as a Hector the Corrector. Your child may feel the need for exactness, to demonstrate that he knows more than someone else, or to prove that someone else is wrong. Using this phrase will:

- Teach your child that a need for exactness is not necessary in most social situations. For example, it is not okay when someone says it is 3:15 and your child responds, "well, actually...it is 3:13;

- Demonstrate to your child that if the words "well, actually" are forming in his brain, it is time to freeze those words and not say what he is about to say. It is likely an unnecessary correction and will only serve to irritate other people and/or make them feel badly about themselves; and,

- Help your child consider whether it is more important to be right or to be happy in his relationships. Emphasize that "almost right" is okay sometimes.

Coaching Example
I guess I did mispronounce that and now I feel a little embarrassed and, honestly, somewhat annoyed. Do you think that was a necessary correction or might that have been better left unsaid to spare my feelings?

15

Sportsmanship

Phrase: *Is Winning More Important than Friendship?*

Maybe you have a child with an intense need to win. This desire to win can undermine her ability to play well with other kids and sabotage her friendships. This can also cause your child to resort to cheating, being a poor winner or base her self-worth on whether or not she wins or loses. Using this phrase can help her understand:

- That the intense need to win can lead to her being excluded and not well-liked by her peers;

- That there is a time and place for that level of competition (such as the Olympics) but, predominantly, she should be playing at a more "friendly level;" and,

- Why someone does not want to play with her. Pointing out to a child that she is sabotaging a friendship by choosing to win over playing fairly, and letting her experience the consequence of that choice, can sometimes bring the point home much more effectively than discussion.

Coaching Example

The reason that your friend stopped playing with you is that it wasn't fun anymore. If you choose winning over friendship, this is what will happen. What can you do to help yourself play for fun and not be quite so competitive?

116

16

Which Thoughts Should Be Shared

*Phrases: Containerize Your Thoughts,
Your Thoughts Are Leaking, or Bubble Thoughts*

Your child may feel the need to express every thought in his head, even if no one is listening. He might not be aware that all of his thoughts are being spoken out loud. He might say things he is thinking that could hurt someone else's feelings, or make unnecessary noises such as humming. Giving your child the image of a container for his thoughts will:

- Help him learn to consider what thoughts should be shared and what thoughts to keep in his head. This is similar to, "If you can't say anything nice, then it is best not to say anything at all;" and,

- Prevent your child from wearing out peers with a constant flow of words. You can suggest that your child think about whether or not his thoughts (or noises) are leaking and whether he thinks the other person wants to hear them. Negative thoughts about others may also be described as a "bubble thought" or a "quiet thought" versus a "spoken thought."

Coaching Examples

Telling your friend that his haircut looks funny should have been a bubble thought. It really hurt his feelings.

I noticed that there are an awful lot of thoughts leaking out and it's becoming too many for me to listen to. Let's figure out how to keep some of those in a container in your brain.

117

17

Kids Who Play Alone

Phrase: Invite Someone to the Party

Your child may have a terrific imagination and spend a lot of time engaged in imaginary play alone. Use this phrase to encourage her to move from solitary play to interacting with peers. This phrase can:

- In a very short period of time, move a child from solitary play to inviting other children to engage; and,

- Provide a fun way of getting your child to "party" with others in an interactive way.

If your child is reluctant, help build the party around her by starting a fun activity and joining in yourself and then looking around for peers to invite in (if they haven't already naturally gravitated to what you are doing).

Coaching Example

I love seeing how much fun you are having playing with those Lego birds you made. I want to play, too. I think it would be awesome for us to invite someone to that great party in your brain. Let's look around the room and see who else we can invite to join in.

18

Taking Responsibility

Phrase: There is an Important Choice to Make

It is important for your child to understand that he actively makes choices for himself and his friendships. This helps him:

- Take responsibility in his peer relationships. If your child is choosing not to work something out, or choosing to be bossy, he is choosing a negative interaction with that friend. He may possibly lose or harm the friendship;

- Learn not to "bail" on friends. If he chooses to quit during a game, then he might be choosing not to be invited to play that game again; and,

- Begin to develop a sense of "cause and effect" in his relationships with others.

Coaching Example

I'm sorry that your friend doesn't want to play with you right now. I noticed it's because you made a choice to cheat at the game and winning was more important to you. What could you do next time so you don't lose a friend to play with?

19

Resistance to Stopping a Preferred Activity

Phrase: Transitions

Your child may struggle with transitions and being able to disengage from a preferred activity. Teaching her the actual word *transition* and explaining that it means to stop doing one thing so you can move on to the next will:

- Assist your child in being able to manage the disappointment that comes from ending a playdate or fun event;

- Provide your child with a concrete word about what is happening when it is time to come to dinner or leave a preferred activity; and

- Open the door to discussions about how to make transitions easier, rather than fighting with your child. Develop a transition ritual and use it every time. For example: your child who does not have a good sense of time may find transitions are easier when you externalize time with a timer. (There are great visual timer apps on smart phones that you can use anywhere).

Coaching Example

Hey there, I know you're still having tons of fun. I'm letting you know I'm going to put two more minutes on the timer and when it rings it will be time for the transition, and for you to stop playing and get ready to go home.

20

Self-Modulation Skills

Phrase: Too Much, Too Little, or Just Enough?

Self-modulation is a skill that your child (particularly if he has sensory integration issues) may find difficult. Using this phrase can help your child who:

- Is having difficulty modulating his body or voice;

- Needs assistance gauging the appropriate level of silliness or energy in his interactions with others; and,

- Would benefit from a way to think through what is happening in a given situation and adjust the level of his intensity.

Coaching Example

I know that you are very excited and love playing tag. Do you think the level of excitement and how strongly you guys are tagging each other is "too much, too little, or just enough?" Too much? Okay, what are some ideas to adjust that?

21

Attention-Seeking Behaviors

Phrase: Do You Need My Attention?

Your child may be looking to play with other kids but does not know how to join in and ends up doing silly or annoying things to get noticed. These tactics usually do not work for him. Other times, she might be misbehaving to gain attention. This phrase helps:

- Label what she needs verbally in order to prevent attention-seeking behavior; and,

- You as a parent, to manage behaviors from the standpoint from which they are coming. If your child is engaging in behaviors that are annoying others, it is highly likely she is looking to join in the play, or needs something and does not know how to put it into words.

Coaching Examples

I can see that you want to play with Alex, but knocking over his Lego project isn't working out so well. How about offering to help him build or telling him you'd like to play with him?

I think you might be stealing the ball from the other kids because you want to play, but it's making them angry. If you would like to join their game, I can help you do that.

22

Supporting the Socially Anxious Child

Phrase: Are You Worried About Something?

Anxiety can be one of the greatest challenges that your child faces with friendships. Anxiety could be driving many behaviors in your child and it may prevent him from forming friendships. Asking your child if he is worried about something will:

- Give him the ability to give a label to what is going on internally for him;

- Help your child with anxiety-based behaviors that impede friendships (for example, yelling at someone because he is worried that they are coming too close to something he just built); and,

- Give you another way of looking at behavior and how your child is reacting. The best advice? Assume any unwanted behavior is due to anxiety and you can't really go wrong.

Coaching Examples

I can see that you're a little worried that your friend is going to knock down the army guys you set up. He will know not to do that if you ask him not to. How about you share the army guys so that he can set them up, too?

I think you're yelling because you're a little worried about trying something new. It's okay to watch first.

23

Managing Impulsivity

Phrase: Was That an Oops or an On Purpose?

Your child may be impulsive and take action without stopping to think first – a ready, fire, then aim child. Your impulsive child may apologize frequently or have trouble taking responsibility for an impulsive act that went wrong. This phrase:

- Teaches your child the difference between an accident (oops) that requires her help to correct whatever went wrong and something done on purpose which requires her to make a true apology;

- Helps you to point out to others when your child has done something impulsively so they can give her an opportunity to re-think the action.

Coaching Examples

I know that your friend was upset that you bumped her project and it fell off the table, but I also saw it was an oops and that you didn't do it on purpose. The best thing to do is offer to help her pick it up and put it back together.

I know that you wrote that bad word on the board without thinking about it first. It's okay to erase it. If you do it again though, I'll know it's on purpose and there will be a consequence for that.

24

Perfectionism

Phrases: Good Enough or Fail With Flair

The need for perfection can get in the way of friendships, especially if your child is expecting perfection from others. The need to be perfect is also frequently an anxiety-based issue. This phrase works well if your child:

- Has really high expectations of herself or others;

- Needs some assistance in knowing that, even when she cannot get it right, it is okay to make mistakes and even laugh at herself (rather than, for example, crumpling up a drawing in frustration);

- May benefit from support in understanding that being perfect is much too hard (and unattainable) and that it is okay to shoot for good enough or to fail with flair.

Coaching Examples

Model this skill for your child by saying things to yourself such as, "Oops, I messed up my drawing. That's okay, it's good enough," or, "I had to use a little tape to repair that project, but it still looks just fine."

I forgot to go to the store and get something for dinner. I guess I will fail with flair and order us a pizza!

25

Struggles with Compliance or Authority

Phrase: Setting Your Own Limits and Rules

Your child may dislike having limits set on him or being told what to do. Complying with directives becomes difficult. Teaching your child that setting his own limits and making reasonable rules to follow can foster a sense of responsibility. Try this for:

- A child who is often in trouble or being spoken to by adults; and,

- When your child resists being told what to do. You might say, "I'm sure you don't like me telling you what to do all the time, so how can you set the rules so that I know you'll be safe," or, "Can you think of some ways you can set the rules so that I don't have to stop you from playing that game?"

Coaching Example

I know that you guys are enjoying this battling game and running around a lot. The problem is I'm afraid something's going to get broken. I don't want to have to make you stop. What kind of rules or limits can you come up with for the game so that I don't to come over there to stop you and take away the fun?

26

Correcting a Mistake

*Phrases: Let's Have a Do-over or
Back Up and Re-Do*

Your impulsive child might do things without stopping to think of the consequences. Or, if she struggles to regulate her tone of voice, she might say things that are misinterpreted. This phrase:

- Offers your child an opportunity to re-think and re-play an interaction that did not go well (and it can be implemented on the spot);

- Gives you a chance to allow your child to fix whatever happened and teach a better way of handling a situation rather than jumping right to consequences; and,

- Provides your child with a quick solution to a problem when she is having a disagreement with a friend.

Coaching Examples

That sounded a little rude and I don't think you meant to sound that way. Let's start over. How could you say that differently?

Was that one of those things that happened before you had a chance to stop and think? How can we figure out a "back up and re-do" to fix it?

It looks like there's a disagreement over whether your friend is "in" or "out." How about a do-over?

27

Resolving Rather Than Creating Conflicts

Phrase: Remove the <u>You</u>

Using the word "you" in an argument or conflict makes the people in the conflict become defensive. It can also escalate the problem to a level higher than it might have been otherwise. By removing the world "you:"

- Your child will learn how to use "I-based" language instead of "you-based" language which involves finger-pointing and can make the problem worse;

- Gives your child an effective way to stick up for himself in a conflict; and,

- Resolves conflicts more quickly.

Coaching Examples

Instead of calling your friend a cheater, try, "I don't like it when the rules of the game aren't followed."

*Instead of saying, "you're mean" to your friend, try saying, "**That** sounded kind of mean. Did I do something to upset you?"*

28

Listening to Other People

Phrase: The I's Don't Have It

There are times, however, when the word "I" can get in the way of your child's social success. This phrase helps:

- If your child consistently turns the conversation back to herself and her favorite topics and experiences. She may appear very friendly and is often working hard at interacting. One of the best ways to be a really good friend to people is to ask about the other person and then listen with interest. A good rule of thumb is to ask two questions for every statement. Talking only about herself is such a subtle social barrier that she may not understand the impact this has on friendships, and;

- To teach your child the art of active listening skills and remind her to keep the other person a part of the conversation.

Coaching Example

I noticed you've been telling your friend all about your pet. It's time to ask your friend about her pet and listen to her answer. Then I want you to ask her two more questions about her pet before you say anything else about yours. Then say one more thing and ask her another question or let her say something else about her pet to make sure the conversation includes both of you.

29

Specific or Unique Interests

Phrase: Specialists and Generalists

Your child may have a specific topic of interest, passion for something, or a vast knowledge in a certain area. While being a specialist in something can help your child fit in to a specific niche of like-minded kids, the concept of also being a generalist encourages him to:

- Be mindful of discussing a topic in too much detail with peers who are not interested; and,

- Learn a little bit about current peer culture (movies, cartoons, music, sports teams, etc.) so that, when these other topics come up, he can contribute to the conversation.

- Throw out a feeler to assess how much interest the other person has for a given topic. Start with more general information and only give additional specifics if asked. This way he can learn to adjust his conversation accordingly.

Coaching Example

You are such a specialist and expert on that awesome video game, but your friend doesn't play that game. What other topics do you think you could talk about with him so that he doesn't get bored? Maybe you can save that particular game topic for a friend who knows how to play?

30

Grumpy or Angry Kids

Phrase: Cranky Creator or Joy Generator?

The moods we experience have a social impact on others. Have you ever "caught" someone else's bad mood? If your child tends to be moody, it's important to help her understand the impact she is having on those around her. This phrase offers:

- A chance for your child to decide whether or not she needs to excuse herself from the activity or take a break if she is in a grumpy mood;

- The opportunity for your child to feel her feelings without pulling anyone else into her mood; and

- The opportunity to point out to your child that while she thinks everything is going wrong, she is simply caught up in a bad moment. The entire time does not need to be ruined. When she has her "grumps" under control, she can continue to have fun.

Coaching Example

I'm thinking that you might have had a long day at school, but it's not okay to be grumpy at everyone else and creating crankiness. How about you have a snack and a drink, and chill out for a bit? Then come back and play with us when you're ready.

31

When and Where It Is Okay to Say Things

Phrases: Keep It in the Boy Barn
or Close the Girl Gate

Body and bathroom humor is part of normal development for kids. Your child may struggle with where and when this is okay. Bathroom humor will not amuse your child's teacher, but it is okay with a small group of friends when no adults are around. These phrases:

- Give your child license to enjoy body and bathroom humor by telling him that it is okay in certain settings. You can also suggest that he go to the restroom and say his potty words in there;

- Identify what we term "trouble words" such as swearing, or other derogatory terms that might get him into trouble.

- Help your child with knowing how to determine when using this type of humor and language is okay, and when it is not (a very gray area). It is perfectly fine with friends, but not okay if there is an adult or someone of the opposite gender in the vicinity; and,

- Protect your child in the longer term. When he learns that he is always to play it on the safe side and not let that type of play or language out of the barn, it could prevent a larger problem down the road. This kind of talk to a co-worker could be deemed sexual harassment.

Coaching Example

I overheard that. While it is pretty funny, it belongs in the boy barn so that you don't get in trouble at school.

32

Adapting to the Social Environment

Phrase: Be AWARE

Each social venue, such as the library, a classroom, a church, or a sports arena, has its own set of social expectations. Your child may have a difficult time adapting to different environments. Use this acronym to help your child adapt to different social venues:

> A – Always
> W – Watching
> A – And
> R – Reading the
> E – Environment

Coach your child to try and match what she sees everyone else doing in the environment.

Discuss different scenarios and what is and is not okay. Examples could be, yelling at the library or cheering for a sports team.

Coaching Example

When we go to the cookout today, let's remember to be AWARE of how people will be expecting us to act and behave. Try to match what everyone else is doing.

33

Teasing or Annoying Others

Phrases: Nice Gets Nice or Don't Poke the Ogre

Social cause and effect is an important concept for your child to learn. Use these phrases when:

- Your child seems to get a charge out of teasing or annoying others, but then the tables turn and the social interaction becomes an argument or a disaster; and,

- When your child has trouble understanding the impact of his behavior on others and finds that he has no one to play with.

Coaching Examples

When you keep poking at and sticking your tongue out at your friend, that's mean and he isn't going to want to play with your, or he may do something mean back. Remember nice gets nice and mean gets mean.

What's happening right now is called "ogre poking." Grabbing the ball away and laughing is causing your friend to become frustrated and annoyed and he's going to become angry. If you want to play with him, let's figure out a way that will work better.

34

Respect for Others

Phrases: Mine Over Manners

Taking others into consideration while maintaining a healthy sense of self is the hallmark of strong social skills. Try this phrase for:

- Gently but firmly pointing out when something being said or done is rude or disrespectful;

- Pointing out when your child is putting herself first in a situation where it is best to use her manners; and,

- Modeling mutual respect.

Coaching Examples

I noticed that we are blocking the way for people to get by. Let's use our manners, be polite, and move over.

I know that you want to go first, but it's not okay to cut someone in line. We are going to practice not thinking "mine over manners" and waiting our turn.

35

Interpreting and Responding to Social Cues

Phrase: Adjust to the Feedback

Ultimately, adjusting himself to the social feedback that he is receiving is the goal of all the social coaching that you do with your child. Using this phrase teaches him that:

- When he is interacting in social situations, he is always receiving some sort of feedback, either verbally or non-verbally;

- If someone tells him that what he is doing is annoying, then he should listen and stop. He might not understand that what he is doing is annoying, so have the other person identify specifically what it is that needs to stop;

- When someone is looking at him in a bored way, he should change the subject; and,

- If someone gives him a strange look, he should think about what he might be doing and decide if he should change it.

Coaching Examples

I've heard your friend say "stop" three times now. That's feedback. Ask him to tell you what he wants you to stop if you don't know.

I see your friend is fidgeting and looking at his watch. What feedback do you think he is giving you?

Afterword

We hope that this parent coaching guide has provided you with helpful tips to increase the social opportunities and success of your child.

In encouraging you to use these tools and strategies, we thought we would share words from parents of children we have coached or whom we have assisted in coaching their own child.

I just wanted to let you know how well my son has been doing. He has a couple of friends that he has over the house and that he goes over their houses. He also hangs around with several different kids during school and does the typical texting with them. He's comfortable at school and is sharing his thoughts and ideas. He's also becoming more involved in Boy Scouts. It's been a great year so far. Thanks for all your support over the years! ~ L.I.

Picked my daughter up from overnight camp this morning. She's AWESOME!!!!!! She did SO WELL!!!!!!! All the counselors who remembered her from two years ago remembered she was a "mess" two years ago, and spoke so highly of her this year. She was given an award, stood in front of the whole camp, and talked about how camp wasn't about "winning competitions" but about having FUN! I am sooooooooooooooo proud of her. Thank you for helping us get her prepped for camp this year! ~ P.L.

I just wanted to share with you how much fun my son is having this summer. I took 2 days off this summer and the mornings off to take him out on outings (playground/beach/pool). Everywhere we go, he instantly finds a friend to hang out with. He has been doing such a great job at trying to listen to what they have to say/show him, and reading their facial and other expressions to know when they are having fun or when they don't want to play a game. I can also see that he is definitely trying to choose to be nice and control his frustration. More and more I am just standing back and letting him play with his new friend. What a difference a year of social coaching makes! I am so happy with all the help you have been providing and all the pointers that you have given me. I can't thank you enough for all the help! ~ G.M.

Hi, several months ago I asked a question about my son being left out by friends who'd joined the same school as him. I just wanted to say that a few months later your advice was spot-on and really helped me resolve this situation. I bought a copy of your book as well and I used a few of your strategies such as having playdates with a diverse range of people to build up his options for friends to play with, getting him to read the book to see your tips for making friends and joining games etc. The results have been fantastic - he loves school, is never short of a friend to play with, his confidence has increased to a huge degree (and his teacher has commented on it as well) and he has resolved his issues with the friends who were leaving him out. If anything his newfound confidence means that he is usually the one suggesting games for all his friends to play! I can't thank you enough for your advice, it was so helpful and clear and really made sense. Another nice bonus has been that through branching out to support his socializing I've made friends with a broader range of mothers as well which has been great. Thanks again for all your help! ~ Belinda

My son's teacher was pretty amazed at how far he has come in one year socially. He was a pretty angry, rude, often nasty person to the other kids when he started at his private school (often without realizing that he was coming off that way). Now he has a group of boys he gets along with great, one of whom even stuck up FOR my son when another child insulted him. That surprised the bully so much that he walked off! He's been invited to several parties this year already, and has had a sleepover. These are major, major steps for him. ~ J.L.

We wish you and your child a happy journey to friendship!

About the Authors

Donna Shea and Nadine Briggs are both accomplished social educators. They each facilitate friendship groups at their respective centers in Massachusetts. Both Nadine and Donna are parents of children with special needs.

Donna and Nadine consult to schools, parent groups, and human service agencies. They are also seasoned public speakers and travel to bring workshops and seminars to schools, conferences and other venues across the country.

Donna and Nadine are certified in bullying prevention through the Massachusetts Aggression Reduction Center and are creators of the How to Make & Keep Friends Bullying Prevention Initiative to provide classroom training and team building for schools.

We would love to hear your feedback on our book, speak with you about providing programming in your area or keep in touch with you about new books and materials.
Find us on Facebook or:
Email us at: howtomakeandkeepfriends@gmail.com
Call us at: 978/413-1965 (Donna) 978/764-2758 (Nadine)

Also by Nadine and Donna

We would greatly appreciate you taking a moment to review our work on Amazon. We learn a great deal from our readers and your comments!

Made in the USA
Monee, IL
18 February 2020

21961686R00079